THE FEDERAL TRUST
for education & research

pension reform in europe

enlightening the debate on good governance

The Federal Trust for Education and Research

The Federal Trust's aim is to enlighten public debate on federal issues of national, continental and global government. It does this in the light of its statutes which state that it shall promote 'studies in the principles of international relations, international justice and supranational government.'

The Trust conducts enquiries, promotes seminars and conferences and publishes reports, books and teaching materials.

The Trust is the UK member of the Trans-European Policy Studies Association (TEPSA), a grouping of fifteen think tanks from Member States of the European Union.

Up-to-date information about the Federal Trust's publications and projects can be found at **www.fedtrust.co.uk**

ISBN 1 903403 05 7

The Federal Trust is a Registered Charity No. 272241
Dean Bradley House, 52 Horseferry Road,
London SW1P 2 AF
Company Limited by Guarantee No. 1269848

Marketing and distribution by Kogan Page Ltd
Printed by J W Arrowsmith Ltd

Contents

Preface

Sir Brian Corby

The *Pension Time Bomb in Europe*, which the Federal Trust published in 1995, highlighted the magnitude of the unfunded pension liabilities in the Union. We pointed out that with an ageing population the problem could only get worse unless reforms of the pay-as-you-go state schemes were implemented. Our report suggested that the way forward lay in a partnership of modified state schemes and private pension provision for all. A greater role for private schemes with maximum freedom to invest would maximise benefits and enlarge Europe's capital markets.

More recently, the Federal Trust has re-examined the problem in the report *Can Europe Pay for its Pensions?*, which is republished in this compendium. Our general conclusion is that there have been substantial changes since 1995. While many further changes are needed, we believe that these are possible and if implemented it is likely that EU countries will be able to meet their future pension liabilities within the limits of the Maastricht Treaty and the Growth and Stability Pact.

Our report is accused of over optimism by Kees Van Rees, Chairman of the European Federation for Retirement Provision in a conference paper in this compendium. He says that the report rightly points to substantial changes in Sweden and Ireland, which have introduced a funded element into their state pensions. He accepts that these are certainly encouraging, although 'It's a pity that Sweden and Ireland account for no more than 3.36 per cent of the EU population.'

Our report also pointed out that Germany – by far the largest EU Member State – is likely to introduce a privately funded pension system soon. The Schröder government has opted, according to *The Economist,* for a way out of their demographic time bomb by a course which is revolutionary by German standards: a privately funded, though also state-supported pension scheme. In the future, the state will provide tax breaks and subsidies of up to DM 20 billion per year to encourage workers to contribute up to 4 per cent of their earnings into such schemes. In the long term these supply as much as 40 per cent of overall pension income, with 60 per cent still coming from the state, compared with 85 per cent today. This German reform is a big step in the right direction.

It is true that France has postponed radical surgery and that Italy needs to take further measures to follow up the significant reforms already in place. Indeed, in Italy the most difficult changes have already been made. The official figures for hidden liabilities that we quoted were based on 1994 data, and are sufficiently out of date to present an unduly alarming picture. In the progress report to the Ecofin Council on the *Impact of Ageing Populations on Public Pension Systems,* the most recent data shows that Sweden and Italy are now expected to add less than 2 per cent of GDP to pension expenditure by 2030. In the majority of cases, the effects of ageing will now add 3-5 per cent of GDP to pension expenditure. The worst performers are Spain, the Netherlands and Portugal, which show increases of 6-8 per cent of GDP between now and the peak years.

There is therefore no room for complacency. Unless there is in place a comprehensive reform process as called for in our report, there is always the danger pointed out by Commissioner Bolkstein in this compendium that pension payments could turn into a vicious circle. He points out that the Commission is encouraging Member States to set in place a reform process that will address the following challenges:

- Running down public debt at a faster pace so as to lower the interest rate burden and offset increased pension spending.
- Raising employment levels, especially of older workers and women, to reduce the ratio of dependants to active workers.
- Proceeding with further reforms of public pension systems, including moves towards greater reliance on funding.

In order to ensure that all EU countries will take the necessary measures to pay for their pensions, our report emphasised that the comprehensive reform process should incorporate pension policy reform as a crucial part of compliance with the Stability Pact. We proposed that the Commission should be required to issue its own annual report on Member States' progress on the same lines as has been done in meeting the entry requirements to the Euro. It is therefore pleasing that President Prodi has suggested that Ecofin should issue an annual report on progress made by member states in meeting their liabilities.

The recent Gothenburg European Council summit moved in that direction by accepting that a comprehensive approach is needed to meet the challenges of an ageing society. Following the Lisbon and Stockholm summits it has called for a progress report for the Laeken European Council, on the basis of a Commission communication setting out the objectives and working methods in the area of pensions.

Finally, while welcoming the proposed directive on the activities of institutions for occupational retirement provision reprinted in this compendium, it is unfortunate that significant freedom of investment has not yet been introduced. Commissioner Bolkestein says in his conference paper: 'The prudent expert principle has operated successfully for decades and it would be unwise to start telling the trustees and social partners who run pension funds how they should do their jobs'. He quotes the following: 'if pension funds were all in bonds, then the cost of an average pension would be 15 per cent of salary. If pension funds were all in shares then the cost of pensions would be 5 per cent of salary.' However, in the draft directive we see that there is a limit of 70 per cent on equity and corporate bond investing. As Jos Van Niekerk writes in his paper, 'A directive with limitations on this point in soon losing a lot of its attractiveness because, for example, a loss of two percentage points in real returns can, depending on the parameters of the fund, lead to a doubling of pension costs.'

We trust that Commissioner Bolkestein's views will win the day when the draft directive is finally revised, after all, as he says, 'it is up to those managing a pension fund to decide what combination of bonds and shares are best, taking in particular into account the age structure of the members.'

Acknowledgements

The study group membership included

Sir Brian Corby Chairman, Study Group
Lord Taverne QC Rapporteur, Study Group
Graham Bishop European Advisor, Salomon Smith Barney
David Callund Managing Director, Callund Consulting
Stephen Cohen Managing Director, Scudder Threadneedle International Ltd
Philip Davis Senior International Financial Advisor, Bank of England
Richard Desmond Group Treasurer, British American Tobacco
Robin Ellison Partner, Noational Head of Pensions, Eversheds
Elsa Forneno Professor of Economics, University of Turin
Baroness Greengross Director General, Age Concern England
Denis Kessler Président, Fédération Franaises des Societés d'Assurance
Jan Mantel Independent Financial Consultant
Jos van Niekerk European Federation for Retirement Provision
Genviève Reday-Mulvey Chargé de récherche, The Geneva Association
Dave Hart National Association of Pension Funds
James Sefton Senior Research Fellow, National Institute for Economic and Social Research
David Simpson Economic Advisor, Standard Life
Richard Blackman Joint Secretary, Study Group
Harry Cowie Joint Secretary, Study Group

In addition evidence was taken from **Jean-Charles Simon**, Adviser to the President, Fédération Française des Societés d'Assurance and **Dr Klaus Heubeck.**

Members of the study group served in their personal capacities. They do not necessarily concur with all the views expressed in the report, but they do support its general thrust and commend its publication. We are most grateful to them for their helpful contributions.

The Trust would also like to thank Axa, British American Tobacco, Scroder Salomon Smith Barney, Scudder Threadneedle International and Shell International for their support of this project.

Can Europe Pay for its Pensions?

Dick Taverne

Introduction

In 1995 the Federal Trust published its report on *The Pension Time Bomb in Europe*. This pointed out that the impact of current demographic trends on Pay-As-You-Go (PAYG) pensions was likely to be either socially and politically unacceptable or economically disastrous unless there were major changes in policy. Since then the issues have been widely discussed. Pension reform has moved up the political agenda in nearly every EU country. Sweden has fundamentally altered its pension system. Many other countries have made changes to benefits or contributions or have sought to lessen their dependence on PAYG. The Commission now acknowledges that pensions are one of the most urgent problems facing the EU.

But the basic problems persist and in some ways have become more pressing with time. Demographic trends have not changed: the birth rate in the European Union remains well below replacement rates, while the rise in life expectancy is, if anything, more likely to accelerate than to level out. Participation rates remain low. The so-called 'hidden liabilities', that is future deficits implied by a continuation of present pension policies, remain *prima facie* unsustainable and imply dangers for the economic health of the whole eurozone if they are not addressed in time.

We have therefore decided to revisit the problems to see what has been done and what might be done to make them more tractable. In Section 1 we review the current demographic trends. In Section 2 we examine some of the recent reforms and other relevant developments. Section 3 considers the implications of present policies without further reform. Section 4 discusses possible solutions within the PAYG framework. Section 5 looks at the possible role of funded private pensions. Section 6 reviews the Commission's proposals in their 1997 Green Paper and its response to subsequent reactions. Section 7 gives our conclusions; and finally in Section 8 we put forward a scheme for promoting pan-European pensions. Appendix A of this report summarises the main features and some of the more important changes in Germany, France, Italy, the Netherlands and Sweden. We have selected these countries either as of special importance because of the size of their future liabilities or, in the case of the Netherlands and Sweden, because of the specially interesting characteristics of their systems.

Section 1: The Demographic Scene

It is now well-known that Europe is rapidly greying. But trends change; and there is no particular reason why fertility rates in Europe should stay as low as they are. In fact if they did, the consequences would be almost unthinkable. Both Italy's and Spain's birth rate, at 1.3 per woman of child-bearing age, is approaching half the replacement rate. Germany's is not far off. Assuming three generations per century, this would imply that in two hundred years, one Spanish or Italian baby will be born for every 64 born today! Both the UN and the OECD assume that Europe's birth rate will recover. (There is some suggestion that in Britain it is rising again from the present rate of 1.8 per female.) However, in the absence of clear signs of a favourable change, it would be most unwise to base pensions policy on hopes rather than facts. This paper therefore assumes that fertility rates remain constant.

Certainly there are no signs that the rise in life expectancy is slowing down. One Dutch population expert predicts that Dutch babies born in 2010 will live to an average age of 115. Even if recent trends do not accelerate as he suggests, a continuance of the rise of 8 years in life expectancy for men and 7 years for women that took place between 1960 and 1995 will cause a dramatic increase in the number of old people in the relatively near future. An EU report in 1995 predicted an increase by 2025 of 48.7 per cent in the number of over 60s. Looking further ahead 200 years from now, if life expectancy increased by 24 years every 3 generations, then there might on present trends be very few Germans, Spaniards and Italian babies, but their average life expectancy would be over 130. In time there could therefore be more pensioners than workers. Restricting forecasts more realistically to a less distant future, it is still a sobering thought that the ratio of the number of people working relative to those retired is expected to drop from four in the EU today to two by 2040.

In addition, the old need more health care and will increase the demands on other social services. Health spending on the age group over 65 is typically four times that on the under 65s. Indeed OECD calculations suggest that health care expenditures could rise by 1.4 per cent, 1.6 per cent, 1.7 per cent and 1.2 per cent as a proportion of GDP over the period 2000-2030 in Germany, France, Italy and the UK respectively.[1]

The picture may not be quite as gloomy as the statistics suggest. First of all, if there are fewer children, there will be savings on schools and family benefit. Secondly, people will be much fitter at a much older age. (The over 60 world championships 100 metres sprint was recently won in the same time as the Olympic 100 metres in 1896). If people are fit enough and work long enough, the pension problem becomes more tractable.

Unfortunately this would require a sea change in the pattern (or the availability) of work. At the moment old people may be fitter but they do not work longer. There was at one time a tendency in some EU countries, e.g. France, to lower the official retirement age. More recently, most countries have raised it. But whatever the official retirement age, there has also been a trend for people to retire much earlier and indeed there were often incentives to encourage them to do so. Some people have argued that early retirement is one way to reduce unemployment. Others argue that people should be allowed to retire earlier because that is what they want. Whatever the reasons, since the 1950s, while life expectancy has risen by 8 -10 years, the number of men in EU countries still at work between the age of 60 and 64 has dropped from 80 per cent to 30 per cent. In France and the Netherlands the figure is now as low as 20 per cent.

While there is, therefore, no reason in principle why spending on pensions and other forms of social security should rise inexorably, the fact is that on present trends it will. In Appendix B we show tables of the expected increase in public spending on pensions and on social security as a whole until 2040. Although the figures are somewhat dated, the prospect is still one that argues compellingly for drastic and early reforms.

Section 2: Recent Changes

The way in which EU states look after their senior citizens varies widely from country to country. But they all have one thing in common: statutory state schemes, nearly all funded on a PAYG basis (generally referred to as the 'first pillar'), play the largest part in providing pensions. Occupational schemes (the 'second pillar') have an important role in some countries, like the Netherlands, Britain, France and Ireland and are funded in all countries except France. Personal pensions (the 'third pillar'), while generally underdeveloped and relatively unimportant, are beginning to feature more prominently in a number of states. Overall in the EU the first pillar accounts for nearly 90 per cent, the second for 7 per cent and the third for 1 per cent of all pensions.

In the last decade an impressive list of changes have been introduced in the EU, which, as already mentioned, make the projections for hidden liabilities for which the latest figures were produced in 1994, appear rather gloomier than they should be.

(i) Sweden

Possibly the most interesting changes were introduced in Sweden in 1998. They are described in more detail in Appendix A, but it is worth mentioning their main features now because they have already been copied in Scandinavia and offer many pointers to possible reforms elsewhere.

Swedish pensions today are mainly based on a so-called Notional Defined Contribution basis and are linked to lifetime earnings. Most of the pension is financed through PAYG, but 2.5 per cent of income will go towards a funded pension administered by the state, with individuals able to choose their own fund. Pensioners can retire at 61, but will then get a lower pension, or they can work as long as they like with pensions accordingly increased. This is because the level of the pension is based partly on the total contributions paid during working life and partly on the average life expectancy at the time of retirement. It is then linked to national economic growth.

Because the scheme is based on actual contributions, it is reasonably stable and although it is not immune to demographic changes, the effect of a rising proportion of pensioners is partly offset by linking pensions to life expectancy. By applying the principle of 'actuarial fairness' it provides a strong incentive to prolong working life. By linking pensions in payment to growth, it gives pensioners their fair share of future prosperity after they have retired. And it creates a partnership between PAYG and funded schemes, although the funded element is small.

(ii) Actions to Raise the Retirement Age

Several countries have not only raised the official retirement age but have taken steps to reverse the previous trend towards early retirement. Germany has raised the retirement age for women and in 1992 introduced incentives for retirement after 65. They have also reformed the system which provided a flexible route to early retirement, by raising the age limit to 65. The previous government introduced a demographic factor in the pension formula, to provide for lower pensions if life expectancy was higher, but the new government has suspended this for two years while it prepares new proposals.

Italy, which had a very complex system with different official retirement ages under different schemes, has raised the retirement age in the main state scheme from 55 to 60 for women and from 60 to 65 for men. They were perhaps the first to introduce a system of 'actuarial fairness' to provide incentives for later retirement. They are phasing out the very expensive seniority pension, the *pensioni d' anzienità* which allowed people to qualify for a full pension after 35 years' work. Italy's problem is not the need for fundamental reform, because the basic issues have been tackled, but the need to speed up the time table for reforms already in place.

The Dutch have increased benefits under their occupational schemes for those who work after the official retirement age and reduced them for those who retire early. In the UK under reforms passed in 1994 the retirement age for women is being raised from 60 to 65 and there are now provisions for flexible retirement up to the age of 70.

After a spurt of reform in the early 1990s, France has made relatively little recent progress in reforming its pensions. There were drastic and realistic reforms of the basic pension and of the mandatory (PAYG) private sector occupational pension schemes in 1993. But attempts to reform the generous and expensive schemes for public servants and employees of public companies have been postponed. France has some of the lowest legal retirement ages in Europe, with an average (for men) of 50.3 to 59.9 for public employees and 61.2 in the private sector.

(iii) Actions to Reduce Benefits

A variety of other measures have been taken in different countries to lower benefits, either by linking them to prices rather than earnings (Germany and Italy), or by changing the basis on which pensions were calculated (France and Italy). In the Netherlands the government is encouraging the social partners to base occupational pensions on average rather than final salary. The effect has been a lowering of replacement rates. Indeed in Germany the previous government announced that the target replacement rate would be lowered from 70 per cent to 64 per cent over a period of 30 years. This target has been modified by the present government to a minimum of 67 per cent. But most expect it to decline to 60 per cent in time.

(iv) Moves towards Funding

There have been relatively few concrete moves towards a greater reliance on privately funded pensions (except in Sweden and Ireland). The subject has been raised in Germany, where a variety of steps are being considered. These include some funding of the first pillar, plus an encouragement of a privately funded element in the second pillar, with new tax incentives. Proposals for private pensions have been shelved in France, where the Loi Thomas, introduced by the previous government to promote privately-funded pensions, was not implemented and the government has firmly announced that Anglo-Saxon style funded pensions are not the French way. However, there will be an enlargement of a special pension reserve fund with surplus cash from the social security budget. In Italy, progress towards private occupational pensions made possible under the Amato and Dini reforms seems to have stalled. They were to be partly financed from the TFR fund ('*Trattamento Fine Rapporto*'), the lump sum which Italian employees get when they are made redundant or retire. But the necessary reforms of TFR hang fire. Spanish companies on the other hand must fund their occupational schemes externally by 2001.

Perhaps the most important initiative for funding has been launched in Ireland, which, like the Swedish reforms, might be a possible model for others to follow. Irish private occupational pensions have in the past benefited from some of the highest investment returns in the EU and are an example of the advantages of a substantial investment in equities. In 1999 the government announced plans for at least a partial funding of the state pension. One per cent of GDP, plus a tranche of the proceeds of the privatisation of Irish Telecom, have been set aside for the purpose. The fund will be managed by the National Treasury Management Agency and will be invested in the same way as private funds, under the 'prudent man' principle. The declared aim is to secure the pensions of a progressively ageing population.

Apart from moves towards private funding, one should also mention moves to establish a Reserve Fund for public pensions. Such a fund was established in France in 1999 and it is to be increased under the measures announced by the government in March 2000. A similar fund has also been set up in the Netherlands to meet the rising costs of the state pension.

(v) Spread of the Equity Culture

One important factor, which should not be underestimated, is the extent to which the equity culture is gaining ground within the EU. An obvious example of the new rush into equities is the explosion of mutual funds; another is the popularity of the *Neuer Markt* in Germany. This trend may have a decisive influence on private pensions in the longer term. If people are happy to invest their savings in equities, why should they object to equity-based pensions? Indeed it seems the public favours private pensions. While the French government has recently denounced the Anglo-Saxon approach to pensions, an opinion poll showed that 78 per cent of the population favoured private pension funds for employees, with only 18 per cent against.[2]

Further, privatisation proceeds apace in the EU. Companies are increasingly looking to the markets for finance. Hostile takeovers, which were once taboo on the continent, are becoming more frequent - the German market is never likely to be the same again after the takeover of Mannesmann by Vodafone. There is an increasing concern with shareholder value and responsibilities to shareholders. While this does not mean that the Rhineland model or other forms of social capitalism on the continent are being suddenly abandoned, these are all signs that the cult of the equity has become an important influence.

(vi) Effect of the Euro

The process is reinforced by the advent of the Euro, which was always likely to lead to a dramatic increase in the liquidity of European capital markets. One of the major consequences of the Euro is bound to be the removal of obstacles to the flow of cross-border investment, not only in law but in practice. Pension funds in the eurozone were circumscribed by domestic legislation in their freedom to invest across borders, although some member states (Belgium and Spain) have relaxed the rules. Life insurance companies have similar restrictions on cross-border investment and in many cases also have to match assets and liabilities in the same currency, which has meant their domestic currency. Further, many countries also prescribed limits on investment in equities. In practice these limits had little effect, because of the relatively small size of continental equity markets. The Allianz, for example, was not in the past constrained in practice by the 30 per cent limit which German law imposed on equity investment. Had it invested 30 per cent of its assets in German companies, it would have owned nearly all of German industry.

Now the domestic currency is the Euro and the scope, in law and practice, for foreign investment is dramatically increased. In so far as national legislation does not yet reflect the new circumstances, the Commission is determined to remove the obstacles. Already the flow of eurozone investment is growing. When all the obstacles are removed, as they will be, the flow is almost certain to turn into a flood.

(vii) The Effect of the Maastricht Treaty and the Growth and Stability Pact

Finally, there is the effect of the Maastricht criteria and the Growth and Stability Pact. If there are no further reforms of EU pensions, several countries' deficits will in time exceed the limits imposed by the Treaty and the Pact. If this happens, there can be no question of the more prudently managed states having to bail out their more profligate partners. The Maastricht Treaty explicitly rules that out. But excessive deficits in one eurozone state can still contaminate others. Excessive deficits will have inflationary effects. Higher inflation in any of the EU's larger economies would in turn have some inflationary impact on the whole zone, which would lead to corrective action by the European Central Bank through higher short term interest rates. In addition, a risk premium in eurobond markets would also affect countries whose systems were sound, leading to higher long term interest rates and choking off investment. All member states could suffer.

Fortunately, the prospects of this happening are somewhat remote. Not only will strong pressure be exercised on member states through the EcoFin Council which monitors compliance with the Pact, but the market is likely to penalise profligate behaviour well before it constitutes a threat to the stability of the rest of Europe. Borrowing by the errant country will become more expensive. From all sides there will be pressure on governments to behave responsibly. For domestic reasons alone, it is unlikely that the projected hidden liabilities will ever materialise.

Section 3: Implications of Present Policies

In Section 1 (and in Appendix B) we referred to the present projections of future public spending on pensions in Europe if there are no further changes in policy. They do not show a reassuring picture. By the year 2040, as a proportion of GDP, spending is forecast to rise to 12.1 per cent in the Netherlands, 14.3 per cent in France, 18.4 per cent in Germany and 21.4 per cent in Italy. Of our selected countries, only in the UK is the outlook for the taxpayer less gloomy. But that is because fiscal rectitude in the UK has been at least partly achieved at the expense of the impoverishment of those pensioners who depend on public pensions; and even on policies now being put forward, the plight of British state pensioners will still compare unfavourably with that of most of their EU counterparts.

It should be noted, that while overall the figures in the table show the need for further action, the figures date from 1995 and do not take account of a number of reforms introduced since then. The figures for Italy, for instance, now exaggerate its future liabilities.

(i) Generational Accounting

We mentioned that it would be a mistake to ignore the effects of demography on spending on other services than pensions. In fact in recent years, first in the United States and subsequently in the EU, a new method of analysis, generational accounting, has been developed to measure the long term effect of all social spending. This provides a useful context in which the pensions problems can be judged.

In 1996 the European Commission launched a round of studies in member states to measure the kind of redistribution that would take place within the average person's lifetime and between generations over a period of up to 100 years and then to assess the implications for long term fiscal policy. Each study takes into account spending on schools, hospitals and welfare payments generally, such as unemployment benefit and child benefit, as well as pensions. The figures should again be treated with some caution because they assume no change in policies and are based on data from an OECD report in 1995. Many important subsequent reforms have not therefore been taken into account. They are also vulnerable to changes in demographic developments.

However, the UK study, for example, gives a flavour of the wider context in which pensions policy should be judged. Some 80 per cent of redistribution takes place from the middle aged to the young and the old. Spending on the young, on schools and child benefit, is likely to decline; and by the middle of the century, expenditure on welfare transfers generally is projected to decline rapidly. On the other hand, expenditure on health will rise substantially and will almost certainly present a much bigger problem than the cost of pensions. Hospital services provide mainly for the old, two-thirds of them in the last two years of life.

Overall, on the assumptions used, the UK's long term fiscal policy should be sustainable. But if there is some relaxation of fiscal discipline compared to the 1995 projections, for example by linking state pensions to earnings instead of prices and by increasing the proportion of GDP spent on health (which has already been announced), taxes would be likely to rise to 46 per cent of GDP instead of the present level of 36-37 per cent.

This is not the place to analyse the full implications of generational accounting. It does, however, clearly indicate that projections which concentrate on pensions alone are likely to understate, rather than exaggerate, the problems for the public purse. It makes reform even more urgent.

(ii) Implications for Level of Benefits or Contributions

Governments will not be able to ignore the fiscal projections shown in Appendix B, even if due allowance is made for recent changes, and keep both benefits and contributions at present levels irrespective of the effect on public debt. They will not wish to see their budget deficits burst through the limits imposed by the Maastricht Treaty or the Stability Pact and expose them to possible sanctions from their partners. Something will have to give. At first sight either benefits must be cut or contributions must be increased.

a) Benefits

Let us assume that prudence and fiscal discipline prevail and that governments will not permit any further rise in contributions. Certainly if governments are worried about the effect on the competitiveness of industry, as they say they are, they will not wish to add to the heavy social burdens that most continental companies already have to bear, or to the high contributions already being paid by employees.

To illustrate the problem it is worth looking at a model constructed by Merrill Lynch,[3] which assumes that the whole of the EU has one PAYG pension scheme under which everyone over 65 receives a pension.

On this basis in 1990 the average contribution to pensions was 13.76 per cent of salary. This provided a pension which represented 43 per cent of average salary. On the assumption that contributions are held at 13.76 per cent (and that participation rates, the retirement age and demographic projections remain unchanged), this 43 per cent rate would decline to 29 per cent by 2020 and 22.9 per cent by 2030 - a cut of nearly 50 per cent. Although the figures vary from country to country and for different employees within countries, the figures for the EU are a reasonable indication of the size of cuts in benefits required.

This is hardly a socially or politically acceptable result. It would replace the pension time bomb by a social time bomb.

b) Contributions

Let us assume instead that the formidable weight of the pensioners' lobby, or perhaps even more influential, of the future pensioners' lobby, prevails over prudence and concerns about competitiveness and incentives. Suppose governments find it politically impossible to cut pensions and prefer to put up contributions. In France, for example, successive governments have found this the less unpopular alternative. In the Merrill Lynch model contributions would have to rise from 13.76 per cent to nearly 20.5 per cent by 2020 and approximately 25.9 per cent in 2030. Contributions would very nearly have to double.

This is hardly an economically acceptable result. The competitiveness of EU industry would be disastrously damaged. Unemployment would almost certainly rise, making the fiscal burdens even worse. A different approach, or a mix of measures, will therefore be required.

Section 4: Solutions within the PAYG Framework

It may be possible for some countries to solve their problems within the PAYG framework. They may not wish to move to private pensions for political or other reasons. Indeed PAYG may present fiscal problems when birth rates are falling and life expectancy is rising, but one should not forget its special virtues. One of the reasons why governments on the continent have been so reluctant to move from PAYG to privately funded schemes is that they feel that by and large the system has served their citizens well.

First, PAYG is effective in giving wide, indeed almost universal, coverage. While private occupational schemes in the Netherlands reach over 90 per cent of the population, this widespread coverage is the exception rather than the rule. In the UK private occupational schemes cover about 50 per cent, with a further 10 per cent holding personal pensions. In Germany some 56 per cent are members of the various occupational schemes (mostly book reserve schemes) and membership is declining. In Italy occupational pensions still play an insignificant role. In France occupational schemes are all financed by PAYG.

Next, PAYG can be effectively used for redistribution. In many state schemes at least part of the pension is a flat rate benefit, although contributions are wage-related. Low earners benefit accordingly. By contrast, many private occupational schemes which provide defined benefits in the form of a fixed proportion of final salary tend to favour the higher paid. It is true to say that in general, the more extensive a country's reliance on state PAYG pensions, the more generously the less well-off seem to be provided for. We have already referred to the fact that British state pensioners are not as well provided for as most of their continental counterparts.

The PAYG system can also provide a measure of intergenerational equity, although this feature has been somewhat eroded by recent reforms. Where the payment of pensions is linked to earnings, the retired get the benefit of rising productivity and rising living standards among the working population. However, recent moves to contain the costs of pensions have led many countries to link pensions to prices instead of earnings. This means, of course, that compared with workers, the prosperity of pensioners declines.

PAYG schemes are relatively cheap to administer. Because they are compulsory, there are no selling costs. Because there is generally no fund to invest, there are no management costs. There are some funded state schemes, but as they do not offer the beneficiary a choice of investment (except in the case of the 2.5 per cent funded element in Sweden), the management costs are trifling compared to those in the private sector.

PAYG schemes are also portable, at least within the nation state. Although private defined benefit schemes can also be made portable, as they have been in the Netherlands, many of them create complications when an employee changes jobs, whereas the state pension remains unaffected by job changes, except in so far as higher or lower wages or salaries may affect contributions and benefits.

Finally, it is also claimed that PAYG schemes offer greater security than privately funded schemes, because they are not vulnerable to the vicissitudes of the markets. However, PAYG schemes carry their own risk, which may outweigh those of private pensions. Leaving aside the basic stability of markets in the post-war period and the measures managers can take to minimise risk in funded schemes, PAYG schemes are highly vulnerable to the risk of political intervention. We have listed some of the measures taken in the last decade to limit the cost of state schemes. Retirement ages have been raised; the number of qualifying years have been extended; the basis for calculating the level of the pension has been altered to make it less favourable; and the link to wages has been replaced by a link to prices. All of these reforms could be regarded as broken promises, or at least as ways in which the expectations of pensioners have been frustrated. If the PAYG system is to be retained, it will need further amendment. PAYG schemes, therefore, are hardly schemes whose benefits are secure.

However, given the many virtues of the PAYG system and the evident determination of several governments to retain it if they can, we start by examining what can be done to make it sustainable.

(i) The Impact of Improved Participation Rates

The future costs of PAYG pensions will be much more manageable and the dependency ratio's decline will be much slower if there is a substantial increase in the size of the work force through improved participation rates. As mentioned earlier, in the EU as a whole only about 30 per cent of those over 60 are still at work. Further, the average unemployment rate in the EU is still about 10 per cent and the rate of female employment is low compared to the United States. What can be done to improve participation rates?

Everyone, of course, hopes that unemployment will decline; and indeed there are good reasons for expecting that it will. The rate of growth in the eurozone has recovered. In the year 2000 it is forecast to average 3.4 per cent and in 2001 3.1 per cent. Unemployment has come down from 11.6 per cent to about 10 per cent and is forecast to decline further to 9.2 per cent by the end of this year. This is still disappointingly high and compares unfavourably with the United States, but at least the figures are moving in the right direction. Further, labour markets are becoming more flexible (in ways which have been almost completely ignored by the British press). In Germany, for example, there has been a decline in union membership; wage bargaining is becoming more decentralised; and in practice there is now freedom to set wages in former East Germany at some 75 per cent of those in West Germany. The advent of the Euro is accelerating the trend to greater wage flexibility throughout the EU. It is also making competition more intense, which should add to the rate of growth, and is leading to a widening and deepening of capital markets, which should improve the prospects for industrial investment. Venture capital in the eurozone is beginning to take off and should in time have a powerful effect on creating new jobs, especially in the high technology sector, as it has done in the United States.

Finally, the size of the workforce could also be increased by a more relaxed policy towards immigration, since most immigrants are of working age. The political objections and social problems will lead most politicians to rule this particular solution out of court. But an increase in the number of immigrants is almost inevitable in any event and this may offer some modest help in reducing old age dependency.

(ii) Raising the Retirement Age

This is perhaps the most effective step any government could take. Let us suppose that raising the official retirement age actually leads to people retiring later. The beneficial effects on PAYG are obvious. Every worker who works a year longer makes an extra year's contribution. At the same time, by not retiring, he or she saves the need for an extra year's pension payment. Indeed an OECD paper[4] argues that if the average male retiring age in the EU rises to 64/65 (and if female employment also continues to rise at the present rate), the effect would almost completely offset the projected rise in the old age dependency ratio.

The solution therefore seems simple. The practical obstacles to achieving it are substantial.

First it requires a complete reversal of past policies which encouraged early retirement and indeed imposed penalties on staying on at work. French engine drivers, for example, can retire at 50 on 80 per cent of final pay, with similar attractive provisions for other public servants. The Italian *pensioni d' anzienità*, or seniority pension, became payable for many at the age of 52 or 53.

But the tide has begun to turn. In the United States it turned some time ago. There the Social Security Acts of 1983 introduced a slow increase in the official retirement age from 65 to 67. Retirement can begin at 62, but with benefits reduced to 70 per cent of the full rate. There are therefore strong incentives to stay at work. We have already referred to the changes in Sweden and Italy, which have adopted a system of 'actuarial fairness,' whereby benefits paid depend on the amount paid in and on residual life expectancy at the date of retirement and increase with age. Both countries have therefore provided incentives to stay at work. Italy will have a minimum retirement age of 57 and a maximum of 65. Sweden only has a lower limit, of 61. Some similar incentives for some pensioners have been introduced, or are being considered, in Germany, France, the Netherlands and the UK.

There is another way in which a system of actuarial fairness can improve incentives. It is likely to make workers regard their contributions less as a tax and more as a form of savings, because, as with private defined contribution schemes, the size of their eventual pension is perceived to be closely linked with the amount of their contributions.

One should not underestimate the political difficulties of raising the age beyond 65. Because of political pressures, successive French governments have flinched from raising the age at which engine drivers (and others) can retire above 50. Further, with most EU employees leaving work well before the official age, there will have to be a cultural as well as a legislative change. But the problems are not insuperable.

First, any political opposition can be partially disarmed if the rise in the retirement age is introduced very gradually and takes full effect a long way ahead. Secondly, it is clearly much easier to make the change when unemployment is falling, as it is today, than when it is rising. Thirdly, a system of flexible retirement ages, as in the United States, Italy and Sweden, goes a long way to meet objections. If the option for early retirement remains, it is up to the individual to choose whether they want more leisure earlier or more money later. Further, by providing strong incentives to stay at work, there is every reason to expect the participation rate to rise. The OECD has estimated that it could improve participation rates by somewhere between 4 per cent and 9 per cent. [5]

While no one can confidently predict what the actual effect will be, it is worth returning to the Merrill Lynch model. This calculates the results of gradually raising the official retirement age from 65 today to 69 by the year 2030. They estimate that it would enable the average contribution rate to be kept to a maximum of

13.76 per cent until 2020, when it would have to rise to 15.9 per cent, with a further rise to 17.2 per cent after 2030.

(iii) A Mix of Measures

The most likely solutions are unlikely to be tidy or uniform ones. They will vary from government to government and will be determined by a variety of political and economic pressures. France provides a good example. At the time of the Balladur government a limited move to funded pensions was introduced, the Loi Thomas. This was a voluntary scheme with tax relief on contributions towards a funded pension, partly to be invested in equities. The Jospin government has abandoned the Loi Thomas and declared itself against Anglo-Saxon type pensions. It first commissioned the Charpin report, which proposed a number of measures to prevent the inexorable rise in the cost of pensions as a percentage of GDP. This, it said, was set to rise from 12.1 per cent in 1998 to between 15.1 per cent and 16.7 per cent depending on different growth scenarios.

The medicine prescribed was unpleasant: a rise in the pension contribution period and a widening of the contribution base, a large increase in the reserve fund established to cover the expenses of the state pension and a closer convergence of the various public sector schemes with the private sector. As already mentioned, the public sector schemes in France, for example that for engine drivers, are very generous and increasingly expensive and compare very favourably with the PAYG private sector schemes.

The government decided that the Charpin report was too gloomy, since economic prospects had improved, or at any rate that its conclusions were politically unpalatable. It preferred to rely on a separate report - the Rapport Teulade. This solved the political problems as if by the wave of a magic wand: it assumed a rate of economic growth of 3.5 per cent a year until 2040.[6] In these circumstances costs would stabilise without the need to raise the average retirement age. Pensions could even be linked once more to wages instead of prices. It did, however, suggest that the differences between the various schemes should be reduced.

Mr Jospin's reaction, apart from the rejection of private funding, consisted mainly of two parts: The problem of generous public schemes was to be resolved by further discussions and negotiations with the parties involved; and shortfalls in the future were to be covered by increasing the pensions reserve fund, which was to provide a source of funding for the state schemes as a whole. A National Pensions Institute is also to be set up to monitor developments and make proposals for further reform as the need arises. In effect the problems have been postponed until after the Presidential and national elections.

France is perhaps an exception because strong recent economic growth has persuaded the government that it can postpone major reform. A possible guide to the way in which other countries might preserve the PAYG system without breaking the rules of the Stability and Growth Pact can be found in the 'Combined Option Scenario' offered by the Merrill Lynch model already quoted. This proposed raising the retirement age from 65 to 68 and raising contributions from an average of 13.76 per cent in 1990 to 14.77 per cent by 2030. It assumed that the activity rate in the EU would rise from 65 per cent to 69 per cent and that there would be an addition to the workforce in the period of some 5 per cent from immigration. On that basis, on retirement the replacement rate of average earnings would fall from 43 per cent to 37 per cent.

This is hardly a comfortable scenario. The small rise in contributions would still add to, rather than relieve, the strains on competitiveness of EU industry and the tax burdens of employees. The drop in the replacement ratio would be a sizeable reduction in the relative prosperity of pensioners. But the rise in contributions is much less than now foreseen and replacement ratios have in any event started to decline. It is declining substantially in all the countries which have replaced a wages link for pensions with a prices link. It seems one of the feasible options for reform.

Section 5: A Partnership of Public and Private Pensions

(i) The advantages of privately funded pensions

a) The shift of burdens between generations becomes easier to bear

No system of providing for old age can be totally immune to demographic changes. If birth rates are falling and life expectancy is rising, the share of what is available to different generations will shift. If there are more pensioners, they will consume a higher share of the national cake and less will be available for those at work.

However, under the PAYG system each worker has to pay their share to support the current population of pensioners. The more pensioners there are, the more each worker has to contribute and the less they keep. Pensions in a funded system depend on what pensioners themselves have contributed in the past. What they get from the fund depends on how much they put in while they are working, how fast it grows and to some extent on what the rate of return on capital is when the pension becomes payable. This is likely to make the burden of contributions more acceptable, since they are not paid to support an amorphous mass of existing pensioners, but pay for the employee's own future pension. It makes it easier to reduce the consumption of the working population. (Of course, as mentioned earlier, to some extent the same advantage can be achieved by a system of actuarial fairness under PAYG).

One should add that the effects of defined contribution and defined benefit pension schemes are somewhat different, Under defined benefit schemes the pensioner's eventual pension has a less direct link with his or her past contributions because the employer guarantees a fixed percentage of final salary, or average salary as the case may be. If the fund grows faster than the guaranteed pension requires, the employer gets the benefit of the surplus. If it grows more slowly, the employer has to make up the difference.

b) Higher benefits or lower contributions

Under PAYG, if the population is stationary and the age structure is stable, the rate of return depends on the rate of growth of total wages and salaries, that is on the growth of employment and employee earnings. Under a privately funded system, the pot of savings is invested and its eventual value depends on market returns. Even investment in bonds has produced higher returns than those under PAYG in the stable scenario. With a declining workforce the gap between privately invested funds and PAYG grows larger. If the pot of savings in funded schemes is invested in equities instead of bonds, it grows larger still. And even better returns can be obtained if there is freedom for investment managers to invest in equities anywhere in the world. This includes the freedom to exploit the faster growth likely to be achieved in emerging markets than in the more mature economies of the EU and can benefit from different demographic patterns in other parts of the world.

In the last two decades, Irish and UK funds materially outperformed Dutch and German funds. Between 1983 and 1996 the real rate of return achieved in Ireland and the UK was 11 per cent and 10 per cent respectively, compared with 7 per cent and 8 per cent in Germany and the Netherlands.[7] This was because the Irish and British funds invested substantially in equities, including foreign equities, while German and Dutch funds (at this time) were predominantly invested in bonds. (It was also worth noting that this happened during a period when the British economy grew much more slowly than the German or the Dutch). Since then Dutch funds have started investing substantially in equities and their returns have also substantially improved.

The effect of higher returns on the amount available for distribution as benefits, or on the level of contributions required, can be dramatic. The EFRP calculated that on the basis of past performance, the cost over 40 years of a 35 per cent supplementary pension in Germany could be up to 8 per cent more than in Britain and Ireland (13 per cent of salary per annum instead of 5 per cent). More generally, over long periods, contributions can be 3 per cent lower for every 1 per cent extra return. The Commission's Green Paper of 1997 gives further examples of the substantial effect on contributions of higher rates of return.

c) A potentially higher rate of savings and economic growth

It is likely that greater reliance on privately funded pensions will increase the size of the total cake, although one should add that this may depend on a number of circumstances, and is far from universally accepted.

First, private funding is very likely to increase total savings, which tend to suffer if PAYG schemes are very generous. Private savings are then crowded out. Further, if there is a direct link between the amount contributed to one's own fund and the size of one's eventual pension, the contribution is more likely to be seen by the individual as a form of saving. Contributions to pay for other people's pensions are more likely to be viewed as a tax. Savings increase the amount available for investment and tend to enhance economic growth. Higher taxes tend to act as disincentives and hamper growth. The total of savings is therefore likely to be increased.

However this depends whether savings through pensions are extra savings or simply replace other forms of savings. That is why there is a strong case for making the second pillar compulsory (if the payroll taxes are not already overlarge), which almost certainly increases total savings as it reaches parts of the population which do not otherwise save, or for a system like that of the Netherlands, where all employees have to contribute if employers and unions in a particular industry agree that a scheme should be formed.

d) The effect on capital markets

A major shift to privately funded pensions would greatly increase the liquidity and depth of European capital markets. The European Commission's Green Paper on pensions of 1997 estimated that pension assets, then some 1,200 billion Euros, could easily grow to some 3,000 billion Euros if they grew to only half the current (1997) coverage achieved in the UK and the Netherlands. If this happened there would be a greatly increased supply of capital which would reduce the cost of equity financing for companies. This would increase industrial investment.

It would also act as a spur to innovation. One of the reasons for the dynamic development of the high technology sector in the United States has been the availability of venture capital for new companies supplied by US pension funds. These have invested an average of 2 per cent of their funds in venture capital. New companies have also made a disproportionately high contribution to the creation of new jobs.

As capital markets become more liquid, the interest rate on corporate bonds is also likely to drop, which will further encourage corporate investment. The more efficient allocation of capital resources will be enhanced.

Overall, therefore, the economic advantages of a move to privately funded pensions can be substantial.

(ii) The disadvantages

The balance of advantage is, however, by no means entirely in favour of private funding compared with PAYG. The merits of PAYG have already been referred to in section 4 above. But private funding also has a downside. Apart from political objections to the Anglo-Saxon equity culture, opposition to private funding has mainly concentrated on two issues: the risks employees may have to bear of a stock market decline or collapse; and the problem of transition and double payment.

a) The risks of private funding

At first sight privately funded pensions offer greater security against political interference. State funds will be dealt with by governments as they think fit. Private savings, like private property, are relatively free from government depredations. The proposition has some force but ignores the potential impact of tax changes. (It was calculated by the Institute of Actuaries that recent changes in the tax treatment of pension funds in Britain reduced their average annual return by some 0.5 percentage points). However, the main risk to private pension funds, like other forms of private savings invested in the market, comes from their dependence on the value of stock markets at the time when savings have to be realised. This, it has been argued, adds an element of luck to the returns from defined contribution schemes, the most obvious and increasingly favoured form of private pension. Two people retiring in subsequent years may get widely different benefits, if markets have risen or fallen strongly in between. Secondly, their benefits depend on the rate of return on capital at the time of their retirement. Those who take out an annuity in Britain today, for instance, may well receive a lower annuity than those who took their pension 3 years ago when interest rates were higher. Fortunately there are a variety of ways in which the element of chance in defined contribution schemes can be substantially reduced.

Defined contribution schemes can be modified to include a basic minimum guarantee, which can be achieved by a change of investment, as the realisation period nears, to a portfolio with a higher proportion of fixed interest securities which minimise risk. Further, periods of low interest rates are generally periods of higher than average equity returns. Therefore what the annuitant loses on the swings of lower interest rates he has usually gained on the roundabouts of a higher value of the fund from which the annuity is bought.

b) The problem of transition

This is much the most serious problem of a move to private pensions and may well restrict the scope of change. Those who retired under a PAYG regime will continue to depend on contributions from the current workforce. If those at work must also provide part of their own future pension by their own contributions, there will be an extended period, until the changeover is complete, during which employees will be paying twice.

Some have argued that the problem can be exaggerated. For example, Professor Borch-Supan of Mannheim University has argued that if the current PAYG system in Germany was frozen, a new funded system could absorb the cost of an ageing population over the next 25 years. The extra costs of transition would be for a relatively short period and would be low, while there would also be compensating gains. The Association of German Banks has also argued that the gains outweigh the problems. Some years ago the Dutch Central Planning Bureau advocated a combination of a rise in the official retirement age with a gradual introduction of 3 per cent contribution rate for private pensions, which, they argued, would enable the contribution rate to be kept stable.

It seems hard to make confident predictions of the likely extra costs and benefits. They will depend crucially on the return that can be achieved on assets and the growth in productivity in the economy. How far extra burdens, if any, would be acceptable also depends on nature of the PAYG system in force in a particular country. But if one looks at end results, the system established in the Netherlands seems to provide a successful model of combining state and private provision.

(iii) The example of the Netherlands

In the Netherlands the largest proportion of retirement income derives from a flat rate basic pension. Over 90 per cent of the population is also covered by private occupational pension schemes, mainly provided by industry-wide pension funds administered by the social partners or through company-sponsored funds. A sizeable proportion of the remainder are covered by individual pension schemes. Regulation is based on the 'prudent man' rule. The result is consistent with the continental ideal of solidarity and avoids poverty in old age. At the same time reliance on privately funded pensions, which provide over 30 per cent of retirement income, at least partially avoids the fiscal consequences of an ageing society. Finally, the very high level of pension fund assets, increasingly invested in equities, achieves the many economic advantages of private funding which have been set out in (i) b-d above. Indeed the Dutch may also have a lesson for British occupational pensions because they have shown that public service pensions can also be successfully funded. The Dutch model combines equity with efficiency.

Section 6: The Commission's Proposals

The European Commission has always been acutely conscious of the problems which recent demographic trends have posed for systems based on PAYG and of the potential advantages of privately funded pensions. In the early 1990s it published a draft directive which proposed *inter alia* that pensions funds should be allowed to choose a manager from elsewhere in the Union, provided they were licensed in their home state, and that fund managers should have freedom to invest in whatever markets they wished, subject to prudent limits.

The directive was nearly a disaster for those, like the Commission, Britain, the Netherlands and Ireland, who wanted to liberalise the rules governing fund management. A majority of states instead wanted the pension and insurance regimes to be the same, with strict requirements for currency matching, and it looked as if their version of the directive might be enacted. This would have tightened, not relaxed, the rules for pension funds and would have extended barriers on cross-border investment instead of abolishing them. To prevent this the directive was withdrawn. An attempt to achieve a similar result by a subsequent Communication was successfully challenged in the European Court of Justice. It was annulled on the grounds that it was intended to impose new binding obligations on member states.

In 1997 the Commission tried again and published a Green Paper on supplementary pensions. The scene had changed significantly since the earlier draft directive. The Euro had arrived, which made currency matching in domestic currencies an anachronism, at least within the eurozone. There was now a wider awareness of the need for reform and a greater willingness in some countries to look at supplementary funded pensions as a way of mitigating the pressures of demographic trends on PAYG.

The Green Paper starts by stressing that basically pensions are a matter for nation states. But freedom to operate and invest across EU borders is a concern for the

Commission. The looming problem of hidden liabilities is also clearly of concern to the whole of the EU. The Commission is eager to create the right conditions for the expansion of private pensions, which it argues could bring great economic benefits for the whole EU. The Green Paper therefore steers a careful course to avoid appearing to impose its own solutions, in a field where member states have jurisdiction and where many take a different view from the Commission, while still making the case for private pensions.

While the Green Paper acknowledges the central role to be played by the state, it accepts the argument that investing private pensions in equities, at least on the basis of past performance, can lead to lower costs or higher benefits and is less vulnerable to demographic changes. It echoes the argument made by the European Federation for Retirement Provision that different rates of return can have a huge impact over a working life on the size of contributions or benefits. 'Assuming the target is a fixed supplementary pension of 35 per cent of salary on a 40 year working life. If the real rate of return on assets is 6 per cent, the cost is 5 per cent of salary; all other things being equal, if the real rate of return is 4 per cent, the cost is 10 per cent of salary, and if the real rate of return is only 2 per cent, the cost is 19 per cent of salary.' It goes on to stress that it is not of course advocating any particular investment strategy for pension funds.

It follows, however, the Commission argues, that fund managers must have freedom to invest. They should not be subject to quantitative restrictions. Such restrictions, by limiting the freedom to spread investment, can actually increase risk, especially if they force investment in government bonds whose value can fluctuate with changes in interest rates. Hence the need for relying on the principle of 'the prudent man'. Further, any obstacles to cross border investment are incompatible with the Treaty of Maastricht.

The Green Paper also emphasises the impact the growth of financial assets will have on EU capital markets. This is likely to be significant but gradual. The supply of government bonds is unlikely to match the growth in funds; hence the need for more equities and also for new corporate bonds. A greater supply of funds for equities would facilitate privatisations, encourage EASDAQ and investment by smaller companies. There are also benefits to be gained from the development of a new corporate bond market, which is underdeveloped in the EU compared with the US, where the market is more than seven times larger.

The Green Paper has not yet led to the publication of a new draft directive. As might have been expected, some of its proposals and observations appear to have been greeted in some quarters with well-concealed enthusiasm. Some respondents felt that more emphasis should have been put on the social solidarity, others on the security aspect of pensions.

It seems that the Commission will press ahead, but very circumspectly. It will retain the objectives of freedom of investment and management. It is determined to remove remaining obstacles to cross-border investment. But it will place greater stress on fund security, compliance with basic prudential requirements and the need to avoid any distortion of competition between the main operators in the supplementary pensions field. In its Communication on consultations on the Green Paper, it has also said that it would be more ambitious in creating the conditions necessary for cross-border membership of pension schemes. We return to this topic in our final Section.

Section 7: Conclusions

The question posed in this paper is whether Europe can pay for its pensions. The answer, we believe, is likely to be Yes. Many changes have been introduced. Many more are in train. They vary from country to country and embrace reforms of PAYG schemes, new initiatives for private schemes and measures to improve economic growth. The proposed solutions are not easy or complete. In three of the biggest countries, Germany, France and Italy, there will in our view have to be substantial further changes if future burdens are to be sustainable. But we believe that in the end the hidden liabilities will be met within the Maastricht criteria and the requirements of the Stability and Growth Pact. This belief is based on the following grounds:

First, there are reasonable prospects that we are entering a more favourable economic climate which will make the problems easier to solve. By historic standards growth rates in the EU in the last ten years have been disappointing. In the last 5 years the United States has far outstripped the EU. In the previous 15 years the EU outperformed America, both in growth rates and job creation. There is no reason to think that the EU must lag behind America for ever or that present rates of unemployment are irreversible. They are already falling. In so far as inflexibility of labour has aggravated EU unemployment, the Lisbon Summit was a major step towards deregulation and greater flexibility. Indeed the supply scene is already changing, as mentioned in Section 4, and the Euro is likely to increase pressures for change, as well as for more competition, rationalisation and industrial investment. One does not have to make the wildly optimistic assumptions of the Teulade report, of perpetual 3.5 per cent growth for 40 years, to argue that faster growth should help to temper the wind to the shorn lamb. A growth rate of 2 - 2.5 per cent may well be attainable, even in the mature economies of the EU with a gradually declining workforce.

Secondly, there are grounds for believing that, quite apart from lower unemployment, participation rates will rise. There is ample scope for greater female participation in the workforce in many EU countries. There is likely to be a greater demand for older workers as the supply of young workers dries up. Perhaps most important of all, because of changes already introduced, the average age of actual retirement now seems to be rising after many years of decline.

In the 1970s and 1980s, not only was the official retirement age reduced in some countries, but there were over-generous schemes for earlier retirement. Staying at work was penalised because it brought no benefits. This was partly thought to be a way of reducing unemployment. Now schemes have become less generous. The DRV (*Deutsche Rente Versicherung*) in Germany, for example, expects the average age of retirement to rise by 2 years because of the gradual effects of the 1992 reform. Older people in Germany still save, which implies that their income is greater than their needs. But if their retirement income drops, those who may not wish to reduce their savings may decide to work longer. Actuarially fair schemes have been introduced which provide positive incentives for staying at work and these seem to be setting a new trend. The effect of all these changes will almost certainly be to raise the effective date of retirement.

Thirdly, if one looks at actions taken by various governments over the past decade, the record overall is impressive. The official figures for hidden liabilities that are quoted date from 1994 and are already sufficiently out of date to present an unduly alarming picture. This should not lead to complacency, but contradicts the scare scenario frequently conjured up by eurosceptics in Britain, that fiscally responsible nations will end up paying for other countries' profligate pensions.

It is true that France has postponed radical surgery, that Germany needs fairly urgent action to stop further rises in its pension costs and that Italy needs to take further measures to follow up the Amato and Dini reforms. But none of these countries have shirked reform in the past. In Italy the most difficult changes have already been made. German governments are fully conscious of the consequences of ever rising labour costs. It seems very likely that they will introduce a form of privately funded pensions. At some stage the projected deficits of the public sector schemes will force France as well as Germany to face reality. As already observed, if inaction causes a rise in budget deficits, or leads the markets to anticipate a rise beyond the limits of the Pact, market pressures as well as possible action by EcoFin are likely to force governments to act. The history of the struggle to qualify for Euro entry shows how effective external pressures can be.

It is not for us to recommend particular solutions, which depend on national circumstances. We have noted many examples of effective changes. The Swedish reforms are one obvious model, which combine a radical restructuring of the PAYG scheme with an element of equity funding. Funding of the First Pillar, as in Ireland, is another example, in our view, of good practice that others may follow. As for those who reject any element of private funding, they may be able to combine a mix of measures as set out in Section 5.

We, like the Commission, see many advantages in a partnership between the public and private sector, particularly where it combines a decent basic minimum provision for all pensioners through a state pension with the advantages of equity funding, as in the Netherlands. The economic advantage of investment in equities has been proved in the past. We recognise that the past may not be a good guide to the future. An ageing society may mean slower growth. The funded pension schemes of the UK, the Netherlands, Switzerland and the US all have the same age profile as the unfunded schemes, which means that many of them will become net sellers of assets when their schemes mature. All these factors suggest that future rates of return will be lower. Indeed insurance companies have all based their future projections of growth on lower earnings on investments.

However, in Britain these projections still expect the return on equities to exceed that on bonds by some 2 per cent, with an overall gross rate of return on equities in the region of 8 per cent. While this is substantially less than the real rates of 10 per cent or more achieved by British and Irish funds in the period between 1983 and 1994, it is still likely to exceed the rate of return on PAYG schemes by a considerable margin. If the real rate of return is some 6 per cent, this would correspond with the highest of the three rates given as an illustration in the Commission's Green Paper how good returns on equity investment can lower the cost of contributions. It still therefore seems justified to expect that equity returns will be high enough to make a gradual replacement of part of PAYE by private schemes worthwhile.

We have concluded that in all likelihood EU countries will take the necessary measures to enable Europe to pay for its pensions. However, to ensure that budget discipline is not threatened by irresponsible governments, it seems to us vital that pensions policy is regarded as a crucial part of compliance with the Stability Pact. President Prodi has suggested that EcoFin should issue an annual report on progress made by member states in meeting their liabilities. We strongly endorse that suggestion. Indeed we further suggest that the Commission should be required to issue its own annual report on member states' progress, on the same lines as its periodical reports in the past on progress in meeting the entry requirements for joining the Euro. Only if it is formally recognised that pensions policy is basic to the EU's economic health can we be sure that the pension time bomb will be effectively defused.

Section 8: Pan-European Pension Schemes

For many years there has been pressure for Pan-European pension schemes. These are now frustrated because employees who work in one EU country cannot deduct tax from contributions paid to a pension scheme of which they are members in another EU country. There would be obvious benefits if such deductions were allowed. It would promote labour mobility and end the discrimination from which migrant workers now suffer. It would greatly benefit corporations which operate across EU borders, the number of which is increasing all the time, by lowering their costs and reducing complexity. It would widen choice for employers and employees. It would be a spur to more private sector pension schemes. Finally, Pan-European pension schemes could provide a competitive benchmark by which other schemes could be judged.

For that reason, in our previous report of 1995, we proposed that the EU should adopt a new Pensions Directive to allow the establishment of a European-wide pension scheme. Although the Commission has expressed support for this aim, it has so far foundered on the need for a degree of tax harmonisation, which remains one of the most contentious issues in the completion of the Single Market.

(i) A New Proposal

We now make a more modest proposal as an interim measure, namely that the Commission should encourage by every possible means bilateral or multilateral tax treaties between EU member states who agree to recognise the tax deductibility of pension contributions of an employee working in one of the signatory countries while a member of a pension scheme in another signatory country.

We suggest countries should allow reciprocal tax deductibility of contributions to pension schemes which are recognised in the home country, up to an agreed maximum of salary, and should mutually agree to recognise all schemes which meet a common set of criteria. Indeed there would be no reason to exclude from such treaties other non-EU countries with funded schemes, like Switzerland and the United States. The common criteria could in time form the basis for genuine pan-European pension schemes.

A model for such bilateral arrangements already exists in the treaty between the United States and France. This provides that 'Contributions paid by or on behalf of an individual resident of a contracting state, who is not a citizen of that state, to pension, profit sharing or other retirement plans that are recognised for tax purposes of the other contracting state, will be treated in the same way for tax purposes in the first mentioned state as contributions to pension, profit sharing or other retirement plans that are recognised for tax purposes in that first mentioned state. There is a further proviso 'that the competent authority of the first mentioned state agrees that the plans correspond to pension, profit sharing or other retirement plans recognised for tax purposes in that state.' This model could readily be adopted between EU countries.

(ii) Proposed Common Criteria for Reciprocal Tax Recognition

The countries concluding tax treaties may well seek to set their own criteria; but the Commission could, by making specific recommendations, help to create certain common criteria to form part of all the reciprocal arrangements. We suggest that such criteria should include the following:

Sponsor: Any employer with more than 20 employees should qualify, whether a corporation, government, Co-operative, charity, club, etc.

Beneficiaries: Any employee would qualify who was a member of a recognised scheme in one signatory country while working in another signatory country for more than a 6 month period.

Benefits: Schemes could be either Defined Benefit (DB) or Defined Contribution (DC), or a hybrid scheme, and could be contributory or non-contributory.

Tax Status: All contributions by employers and employees should be tax deductible. Countries may well wish to limit the amounts that can be deducted, at perhaps some 15 per cent of a year's salary.

Funding: An actuarial valuation by an authorised actuary should be required for all DB schemes to ensure solvency and to limit overfunding.

Control: A qualifying pension scheme should meet the criteria in the country of establishment with respect to governance and prudent investment.

Appendix A: Country by country Review

This review does not provide a comprehensive picture of the pensions regimes of the selected countries. It is concerned to highlight the most important features of their current regimes, and of recent or proposed reforms, which are relevant to the question posed in this paper, namely whether the countries concerned can pay for their pensions in the future or whether their pension liabilities are likely to increase their public debt in a way that would cause embarrassment to their EU partners.

1) Germany

Germany has a generous PAYG state pension system, which provides about 82 per cent of pensions paid, of which some 12 per cent consist of pensions paid to civil servants. Benefits aim to provide a replacement rate of 70 per cent of the net average salary of a comparable worker. Occupational pensions take four different forms, the most important of which is the book reserve scheme, whereby the employer agrees to pay the employee a retirement pension backed by reserves on the company's balance sheet. The form of occupational pension closest to privately funded schemes elsewhere is the *Pensionskasse*, which are in effect private insurance companies set up by a larger group of companies with contributions shared between employers and employees. However, occupational pensions altogether account for only 5 per cent of retirement income, compared with some 20 per cent in France, 25 per cent in the UK and about 36 per cent in the Netherlands, and are declining even further. The Third Pillar consisting of personal pensions under private insurance contracts accounts for the remainder of retirement income.

With a low birthrate in Germany, at some 1.4 per cent per female of child-bearing age, and a fast rising percentage of old people, pension contributions are due to rise to an intolerable level unless there are further reforms. At present pension contributions are at 19 per cent of earnings (after taking account of a sizeable subsidy from general taxation). The figure is expected to rise to some 28 per cent by 2030. On top of this there are heavy costs for health, unemployment insurance and long term care.

The last major reforms were in 1992, when the pension was linked to net wages, the retirement age for women, the unemployed and the long term insured was raised for all to 65 (in stages), and, perhaps most important of all, incentives were provided to continue working until the formal retirement age. This reversed the earlier trend towards ever earlier retirement. Further reforms were proposed by the last government to introduce a demographic factor by relating pensions paid to life expectancy. The aim was to reduce the replacement rate to 64 per cent and keep the future rise in pension contributions to 24 per cent. But these proposals were not accepted by the new government. New discussions were started to achieve agreement on further reforms, while an interim measure was adopted to limit increases for pensions in payment to the cost of living for the years 2000 and 2001.

Interestingly, it now seems to be agreed that a funded element should soon be introduced into the state system. It is likely to be small, perhaps 2.5 per cent. It is not yet known what the total contributions to the state scheme will then be, whether the funded element will be mandatory or compulsory, whether there will be tax incentives, who will manage the funds or how they will be regulated. But it will almost certainly be a major step forward. There are also discussions of promoting a privately funded element in occupational pensions.

Even these reforms are unlikely to be sufficient in the longer term. It seems that in time there will have to be some adjustment in the official retirement rate, or further action to encourage later actual retirement and some lowering of the replacement rate.

2) France

Pensions in France are almost entirely based on PAYG (the self-employed are one of the few exceptions) and the Jospin government has decisively rejected moves to introduce privately funded pensions. The system is extremely complex, with a great variety of schemes, and favours public service employees, who benefit from a lower retirement age and in time will also have a higher replacement rate.

Those in the public sector, who constitute 21 per cent of the population, are subject to 18 different special schemes; the 'regime general' applies to all private sector employees; and those in the private sector are also subject to two compulsory additional private schemes, ARRCO for all employees and AGIRC for those in managerial positions. The schemes are all jointly run by employers and unions. The retirement age (for men) is 61.2 for private sector employees and varies for public sector workers from just over 50 for railway employees to just under 60 for those in local government. Penalties for early retirement are much tougher in the private sector. Pensions are income related and replacement rates seem difficult to calculate , but vary between about 55 and 76 per cent. As a result of the Balladur reforms of private pensions in 1993, when the contribution period was lengthened and the calculation of benefits was made less favourable, the replacement rate will decline fairly sharply in the next 40 years. According to the Rapport Charpin, by 2040 it will vary from 40-52 per cent in the private sector, to 57-58 per cent in the public sector.

Unless one takes a very optimistic view of future growth rates, the cost of pensions will rise to 15-17 per cent of GDP by 2040 if all pensions are indexed to prices, and to 20 per cent if indexed to wages. Although public sector employees number less than a quarter of the total, their pensions will account for over 50 per cent of the total deficit of the whole system.

Relatively little progress has been made in reforming the system since the Balladur reforms. Even then the attempt to limit the cost of public sector pensions was defeated by a series of strikes. The recent Rapport Charpin, from the head of the Commissariat du Plan, which recommended *inter alia* a further lengthening of the contribution period and bringing the public sector more in line with the private sector, has been largely shelved. The government preferred to act on a report from the Economic and Social Council, the Rapport Teulade, which argued that 3.5 per cent growth over the next 40 years avoided the need for unpleasant measures and would enable pension increases in future to be based on wages rather than prices. Its assumptions have been widely regarded as exceedingly optimistic.

The Jospin government announced three measures in response to this report, only one of which was a concrete reform. First, discussions should take place with the public sector to agree a pact on the reform of their pensions. The pension organisations themselves should propose the necessary solutions. Secondly, a Pension Advisory Council would be set up, made up of the social partners, Parliament and specialists, which would monitor developments and make proposals as necessary. Thirdly, the reserve fund established in 1999 to fund the gap in future funding of state pensions is to be strengthened. It will get additional funds from various surpluses in the budget and will be capitalised to build up further income from the fund's assets or possibly from future privatisations.

It seems that a more realistic approach to France's future pension problems must wait until after the Presidential and Parliamentary elections.

3) Italy

Italy has in some ways been a pioneer in European pensions reform. By the early 1990s, its problems seemed among the most intractable in the EU. In the decade after 1980, Italian spending on pensions had doubled while in the EU as a whole they increased by 40 per cent. However, reforms during the administrations of Amato and Dini in 1992 and 1995 put in place a structure which should in time make the Italian system viable. The extravagantly generous seniority pension, the *pensioni d' anzienità* which gave full pension rights after 37 years' contributions, is being phased out, although it still provides 80 per cent of final salary to some people retiring in their mid fifties. The complexities and inconsistencies of the system, with a variety of retirement ages for different categories of workers, have been largely ironed out; and, most importantly, the Italians were the first major country to introduce the principle of 'actuarial fairness' since adopted by Sweden: benefits were to become gradually related to life time contributions rather than earnings and were to be related to life expectancy at the time of retirement. This provides strong encouragement for people to stay at work.

The basis was also laid for private funded pensions. There was to be tax relief for contributions up to 2 per cent of salary (later to be increased to 2.5 per cent) to private schemes and there were proposals for converting the large TFR (*trattamento di fine rapporto*) funds held by Italian companies into capital for private schemes. These funds were originally established as an insurance scheme against involuntary loss of employment and gradually became a form of deferred compensation, financed by a credit of 6.9 per cent of gross wages. They also provide Italian companies with a cheap source of capital.

Despite these fundamental reforms further action is still needed to limit Italy's future liabilities. There was some further pruning by the Prodi government, but even so it is only after 2030 that the Italian system moves closer to a satisfactory balance. There will need to be some further restrictions of entitlement under the seniority pensions and some speeding up of the transition from wage-related to contribution-related pensions. But little progress has so far been made in adapting TRF funds to the needs of private pensions. If these are to play a more important part, as originally intended, it seems new incentives must be provided to encourage switching funds out of the TFR funds, as suggested by Professor Elsa Fornero, and there may have to be some increase in taxation to encourage a partial contracting out of the state scheme.

4) The Netherlands

The Netherlands has the most developed system of occupational pensions in the EU. There is a basic PAYG state pension paid for by contributions of 17.9 per cent of income up to a ceiling. It provides a flat rate benefit of Dfl 21,900 for a single person and 30,400 for a couple (about £9,000 a year). Private occupational pensions cover over 90 per cent of the workforce with most of the rest being covered by personal Third Pillar pensions. These occupational funds are not strictly compulsory, but apply if agreement is reached between employers and unions that there shall be an industry-wide scheme or that there shall be a scheme specific to a particular company.

In practice this means nearly universal coverage. The schemes are administered jointly by employers' and union representatives and provide for investment of pension funds on a 'prudent man' basis, in the public as well as the private sector. Funds have become increasingly invested in equities, with an increasingly beneficial effect on their rate of return, which was 12.8 per cent over the 5 year period ending 1999. The aim is to achieve a 70 per cent replacement rate after 40 years' service, when the state pension has been taken into account.

Despite their heavy reliance on funded occupational pensions, the Netherlands are not entirely free from the problem of hidden liabilities, although these are less onerous than in other countries. They have therefore taken, and are taking, further actions to limit costs and to increase participation rates. Like France and Ireland, the government has also decided to start a Reserve Fund to cope with the subtantial increase expected in the cost of state pensions. Benefits for those who retire early have been cut or have to be financed by higher accrual rates. Pensions rights in occupational schemes are now increasingly based on average rather than final salary; and the automatic link between occupational pensions and the basic pension is increasingly being severed so that pensions are more immediately linked to earnings and do not automatically increase if the share of the state pension's contribution to replacement income declines. There is also a tendency for pensions which used to be defined benefit schemes to become hybrid ones, with a mixture of the features of both defined contribution and defined benefit schemes.

5) Sweden

Sweden changed its pension system fundamentally in 1998 and has provided a system, a Notional Defined Contribution system, that several countries (e.g. Norway and Latvia) have already adopted as their model. It is an ingenious system that combines PAYG and funding, support for the low paid and incentives to prolong working life, limits on future costs and a share for pensioners in future prosperity.

The system establishes a clear link between contributions and benefits, except for the low paid. For them there is a 'guarantee pension', which is means-tested, with other forms of income taken into account. For the rest the size of their pension depends on the contributions made and on their life expectancy at the date of retirement, i.e. 'a fair actuarial system'. Once vested, the pension is linked to average income growth.

The income on which contributions are levied includes income from employment and business activities, as well as sickness benefit and other social security payments, and give contributors a notional claim on the total paid plus interest. The contributions are fixed at 18.5 per cent, of which 16 per cent is used as a PAYG payment to pay current pensions in the same year. The remaining 2.5 per cent, however, is invested in a fund and will earn interest in a premium reserve account. The fund is administered by a state agency, but the individual can choose an investment manager for their premium reserve pension and can have it invested as they wish.

There is a flexible retirement age, with a minimum but no maximum. The minimum age is 61 and those who retire then will have their account converted into an annuity determined as described, on the basis of their contributions and what their fund has earned, plus an assessment of their life expectancy. Those who retire later will score a double gain, not only from longer contributions and the extra earnings of their pot, but from higher benefits because of a lower life expectancy. Everyone will receive a statement annually about their acquired rights and projected pension.

The scheme is being phased in gradually, with the new benefits gradually replacing those of the previous system depending on the date of entry of beneficiaries into the scheme. It is envisaged that the contribution rate will remain at 18.5 per cent and that the system will be financially stable. Although benefits are linked to economic growth, the system is also responsive to demographic changes. However, as it is still a PAYG system, with the state responsible for paying existing pensions out of current contributions, it is not clear that it can be entirely isolated from the budget if the number of pensioners outgrows the new entrants into the workforce faster than expected. But for the transition period, the Swedish government has accumulated large reserves to meet the special demands of the baby boom generation.

The Swedish reform seems extremely well designed both to meet the problem of ever rising costs and to combine the advantages of PAYG with the additional benefits that an element of funding can provide.

Notes

[1] See Phil Davis, 'Population Ageing and Retirement Income Provision,' in *Ageing Societies, the Global Dimension*, ed. B Bosworth and G Burtless, Brookings Institution Press, 1997.
[2] Merrill Lynch Pension Reform in France, April 2000, p25.
[3] Merrill Lynch, European Pensions Reform, 1999.
[4] Maintaining Prosperity in an Ageing Society, OECD 1998.
[5] The Retirement Decision in OECD countries, OECD Working Paper 202.
[6] One might compare the Rapport Teulade with the famous reccomendation of the economist cast upon a desert island with a crate of beans: 'Let us assume we have a tin-opener'.
[7] European Federation for Retirement Provision (EFRP) report, 1996.

Appendix B

Public pension expenditure per cent of GDP at 1994 prices

	1995	2020	2040	2070
Austria	8.8	12.1	15.0	13.5
Belgium	10.4	10.7	15.0	14.3
Denmark	6.8	9.3	11.6	11.7
Finland	10.1	15.2	18.0	17.8
France	10.6	11.6	14.3	14.0
Germany	11.1	12.3	18.4	15.5
Ireland	3.6	2.7	2.9	2.2
Italy	13.3	15.3	21.4	17.0
Netherlands	6.0	8.4	12.1	11.0
Norway	5.2	8.6	11.8	11.1
Portugal	7.1	9.6	15.2	14.8
Spain	10.0	11.3	16.8	16.0
Sweden	11.8	13.9	14.9	15.1
UK	4.5	5.1	5.0	3.1

US	4.1	5.2	7.1	7.4
Japan	6.6	12.4	14.9	14.4

Source: Ageing Populations, Pension Systems and Government Budgets, OECD 1996.

Appendix C

Demographic assumptions and dependency ratios in the EU, 1995-2035

	Elderly Dependency			Oldest-old Dependency			Gross Fertility		Life Expectancy	
	1995	*2015*	*2035*	*1995*	*2015*	*2035*	*1995*	*2015*	*1995*	*2015*
B	39.0	45.3	60.5	11.2	15.6	21.8	1.6	1.8	79.8	81.1
DK	35.2	44.0	51.5	12.3	12.4	16.9	1.8	1.9	77.9	78.0
D	35.7	47.3	69.2	10.8	17.4	24.1	1.4	1.4	78.7	81.1
E	38.1	45.1	74.5	11.1	17.0	26.2	1.3	1.3	80.5	82.4
F	37.1	46.9	62.2	11.3	17.0	24.9	1.7	1.7	81.6	83.2
IRL	30.2	37.5	59.2	9.6	10.9	20.3	1.8	1.8	77.9	81.9
I	39.5	53.0	79.7	11.5	20.6	29.0	1.3	1.5	80.4	83.0
NL	30.5	43.6	65.3	9.6	12.9	23.6	1.5	1.7	80.3	83.0
A	34.7	42.3	66.2	10.7	14.1	22.4	1.4	1.5	79.0	81.6
FIN	34.0	51.7	60.9	10.3	15.6	25.1	1.8	1.8	80.5	82.0
S	41.4	54.9	66.8	15.4	19.5	28.8	1.7	1.8	81.5	83.3
UK	37.7	43.8	57.8	12.9	14.4	20.2	1.7	1.8	79.3	80.7

Source: European Commission

The Need for Reform and a Social Approach[1]

Carlo De Benedetti,

Chairman, Cofide CIR.
Vice Chairman,
European Round Table of Industrialists.
President, Foundazion Rodolfo Debenedetti.

In many European countries, the public pension systems are becoming unsustainable. Despite the fact that the causes and consequences of the impending crisis are very well known, time is running out without any effective reform taking place. Opinion polls show that most people are aware of an incoming crisis (although they tend to underestimate its magnitude), as we can see from a recent survey carried out by *Fondazione Rodolfo Debenedetti*;[2] it is only policy makers who pretend financial distress of pension programmes is just a temporary nuisance. They seem to take the view that the pension bomb will not explode if left untouched.

The problem is acute and widespread in Europe. Five examples stick out: Belgium, France, Germany, Italy and Spain. All of these have in place generous pension programmes, largely based on a Pay-As-You-Go financing method.

Not only Demographic Causes

The 'support ratio' of workers to pensioners is falling throughout Europe, as the baby-boom generation nears retirement, and is succeeded by a smaller generation of workers. Despite the fact that this is fully predictable, almost no attention has been paid to the fact that recent demographic trends directly affect pension expenditure and pension financing (and have a strong impact on health spending and financing too, as emerges from a recent work from the OECD).[3]

What policy makers seem to ignore, or recognise with a considerable lag, is the *permanent* nature of demographic changes. In fact, there are four distinct trends that feed into the pension 'time-bomb':

1. In future years there will be a large number of retirees relative to the working population.
2. These retirees will live much longer than at present.
3. The number of children is falling.
4. Workers tend to retire at much younger ages than previous generations.

We cannot live in the hope that these trends will rapidly fade away. Even once the baby boom generation has fully retired the increased longevity, the tendency to retire early and the reduced fertility will inexorably persist in developed countries, and particularly European countries.

However, the problem is not only with demographics. Excessively generous pension systems, both in terms of eligibility rules and in terms of benefits paid out to retirees are added to it. Generosity of pension systems is more widespread than one could imagine. It is not only the monolithic earnings-related schemes existing in Italy or in Germany that guarantee very high replacement ratios (pension over last wage) to employees and let them out of the labour force at very young ages: even partially funded systems (e.g. the Netherlands) have allowed for large loopholes in their programmes.

Social partners have not always acted in the best interest of workers. Unions often show a 'status quo bias' in dealing with reforms that would rebalance the programme.

Finally there is another dimension to the problem, which seems to have been totally neglected. When the programme is entirely based on a pay-as-you-go system, younger generations will receive very little from the system, while contributions (payroll taxes) are usually substantial. In other words they pay somewhat for their own pension, but mainly for their fathers' pensions. In pure pay-as-you-go systems, still prevailing in Europe, we are asking younger generations to continue to invest in an asset whose return is quickly diminishing or even turning negative. This is the irreversible destiny of systems that are fully exposed to the demographic risk. Many young workers would much rather invest their money elsewhere; this clearly emerges from the Fondazione's survey. Youngsters would like to opt-out from public pension systems. We could adjust for this by diversifying their pension portfolio.

Time is running out

The 'window of opportunities' for reform is already small, and it is rapidly shrinking. The 'baby boom' generations are still in their late forties and fifties and should not have wholly retired for another 10 to 15 years. The cost to society of the demographic transition – higher costs of state pensions, higher costs of health care, and increased dependency – will rise rapidly thereafter. There is a time interval in which policies can be shaped to deal with this different type of society – in which, for example, older workers can be retained in the labour force and encouraged to save for their retirement.

In an era when individuals should be encouraged to work longer, many governments still actively encourage workers in their late middle age to leave the workforce and take early retirement. Until recent years, public policies that directly or indirectly encouraged earlier retirement were not seen as a major problem. Often they were viewed positively because of their alleged effects in reducing the pressure of unemployment. Now the aim of policies must be not only to encourage later, and in some cases, more gradual, transitions from work to retirement, but also to improve work possibilities for the unemployed. For example, in Germany the possibility for people to pursue old age part-time employment has been introduced. This allows employer-employee agreements where employees over 55 can work half time, with wage supplements for employers to compensate both wages and pension contributions. Employers are in turn compensated by the government if the unemployed or new school graduate fills the resulting vacancies.

It is important to place such reforms in context, including the labour market situation. In fact, it is very well known that unemployment in European countries is today mostly a supply problem rather than a demand one. In the core of Western Europe there is a lack of workers rather than a shortage of jobs. These are the ideal conditions under which pensions reforms prolonging the active life can be carried out.

Methods for Reform

The goal should be a more balanced pension programme with a sufficiently large funded component. The major steps to be taken in this respect are:

1. Promote social partnership. Involve workers, government and industry in the provision of income for retirement and encourage reforms that make pension spending more credible.
2. Encourage individual responsibility for retirement saving.

3. Confine the role of public pension systems mainly to redistributing resources from the lifetime rich to the lifetime poor and shift to the other social partners the responsibility for full old-age insurance provision for workers.

There are some success stories on promoting social partnership, for example, the Netherlands where we see that the social partnership has achieved a good balance in terms of combination of public and private provision.

The availability of resources for low-income individuals could be achieved by reducing compulsory contributions to public pensions and providing a solid safety net.

An ageing Europe needs to retain workers in the workforce when they reach the peak of their seniority: pension programmes should no longer encourage early retirement. Retirement age must be flexible, but discouraged below 65.

Pension arrangements should not hamper labour mobility. Workers should be able to move freely across the labour markets. Hence long vesting periods should be avoided (rights to receive a benefit should be made readily available), and the build-up of pension rights should be protected while the transferability of pension rights, both within a country and between countries, should be guaranteed. Most of all, the taxation of pension funds should not be an obstacle to portability of pension rights.

The portability of pension rights and the free movement of workers do not imply an interference of the European Union into personal income taxation; on the contrary, it is in line with draft propositions being proposed by the European Commission.

Workers and firms can join forces and exploit 'global' market opportunities in order to provide a higher standard of living to workers in their old age. It should be stressed that global investment is the keyword to achieve flexibility of pension programmes vis-à-vis demographic and political crises: this is exactly where unfunded pension systems do fail.

Global diversification of resources accumulated for retirement provision can be achieved only if there are no barriers to capital movements within the 'prudent man' framework. Prudential rules are actually inconsistent with national quotas in the allocation of the portfolio of pension funds.

This also implies allowing for greater competition in private pension provision. Hence there should be freedom of contract between sponsoring company and the pension fund and avoiding any automatic cost-increasing mechanism being imposed on pension funds (i.e. automatic linking of benefits to wages, etc.).

Gaining Support for Reforms

It cannot be denied that reforms have a cost, and resistance to change also comes from perceptions that one will be amongst the losers in the transition from the old to the new system. Yet, all generations can benefit from a more balanced (i.e. more funded) pension programme, if the costs and the benefits of pension reforms are shared. In particular, compensation mechanisms can and should be designed to avoid any extra-burden caused by changes in the system that the middle generations will bear. This would help to win support for reforms.

Summary

It is time for Europe to rethink its pensions systems. A co-ordinated action is needed across European countries for at least four reasons:

- Firstly, European countries should be forward-looking and think now about the implications, at European level, of the breakdown of the current pension arrangements.
- Secondly, all over Europe there will be a similar adverse demographic scenario in the next fifty years, to be addressed with a similar set of actions.
- Thirdly, a delay in reforming public pension programmes in one country would become a burden for all the other countries; conversely, a step taken in the right direction has beneficial effects on Europe as a whole.
- Fourthly, an integrated Europe needs free movement of workers and capital, which can be achieved by flexible pension arrangements, allowing for portability and transferability of pension rights across jobs and countries.

Notes

[1] This paper was delivered on the 6th of February 2001 at the one-day conference on the subject of 'Defusing Europe's Pensions Timebomb'. The conference was organised by Friends of Europe with Fortis, Citibank, Deutsche Bank and PricewaterhouseCoopers and in association with Federal Trust and EurActiv.com.

[2] *Would You Like to Shrink the Welfare State?*, by Tito Boeri, Axel Boersch-Supan and Guido Tabellini, available at the internet site of the Fondazione Rodolfo Debenedetti: www.frdb.org.

[3] OECD [2000], *Reforms for an Ageing Society.*

The Urgent Need for Pension Reform[1]

Trevor Llanwarne

Partner, PricewaterhouseCoopers

In this piece I aim to explore the following:

1. Is There a Need for Reform? I believe yes.
2. How Urgent? I believe action is needed now.
3. What Are the Big Issues? I believe the two big issues are setting criteria for future costs and accepting that State Pension Ages need to rise, perhaps to an age of 70, by the middle of this century.

The Impetus for Reform

About 12 months ago, PricewaterhouseCoopers undertook some research on the 'Pensions Time Bomb.' A summary of our conclusions is given in our booklet *The European Pensions and Savings Revolution*. In this booklet we examined the position from now to 2050 in the four largest EU countries: Germany, the UK, France and Italy.

We can start examining the need to reform by looking at the number of workers per pensioner (the support ratio). Currently this is about 4:1 with all countries being at about the same level. Our projections then show this to drop to about 2:1 with bigger drops for Germany and Italy.

No doubt you have heard this before. What does it mean for pension costs? Our projections show that - with no reform, and benefits rising in line with average earnings in the economy - pension costs will rise from 7 per cent to 11 per cent in the UK with earnings indexation, but would rise much less, if at all, with the current price indexation. The rise with earnings indexation is far more dramatic: from 16 per cent to 28 per cent in Germany and France, and from 20 per cent to 47 per cent in Italy. This is the annual percentage share of average workers' earnings needed to provide pensions on a pay-as-you-go basis at current benefit levels.

These are unsustainable costs given that the total social costs (including healthcare, unemployment etc.) will make for a much higher total. Action is required.

When Should Reforms take Place?

Interestingly, the projections suggest that the contribution levels for retirement pensions in these four countries will be reasonably stable from 2000 to 2010. Only in Italy is any material increase projected from 20 per cent to 24 per cent. Even this not very large.

Does this show that we can wait ten years? This is not my belief. By that time it will be much too late. The problem relates to the nature of the changes required. It is very difficult to change the benefits accrued, particularly for older employees. Difficulties arise because of the common philosophy of linking benefits to contributions. This makes the structure seem like an insurance structure. Indeed, it is often called social insurance or national insurance. This 'insurance' presentation means that workers will not accept the reduction in rights already paid for. Changes are introduced either for future years only or for the younger workforce.

So we need to look at the problem another way. We can fix a maximum future cost and then work out how future benefits need to be reduced if action is taken now compared with action in ten years' time.

The results are illuminating. What we find is that the reductions needed are much worse if you wait until 2010. I will provide one more set of figures as an example: If the costs are never to exceed 20 per cent, a reduction of 35 per cent in future earned benefits could be needed if started now in France. If, however, we wait ten years until 2010, a 70 per cent reduction is needed. Germany is not much different and the figures for Italy are even worse.

What do I conclude from all of this? That despite initial appearances, EU states cannot, indeed must not delay. Action is needed now.

Proposals for Further Reform

While it is true that some reforms that should mitigate these adverse cost trends are already in place, our conclusion is that they do not yet go far enough to resolve the problem in countries such as Germany, France and, in particular, Italy. More needs to be done, and to be done quickly.

I would recommend two specific actions:

1. Each state should be set an upper limit on pension costs based on sustainable costs in a globally competitive economy. This should be similar in principle to the Maastricht criteria and based on agreed assumptions for the future.

2. Each state should then put together an action plan to ensure that the limit is not breached in any year through to 2050 on those assumptions. The plan should be reviewed regularly in the light of experience. I suggest every three years.

Only through such an approach can there be a real impetus to address the issues now.

If you examine the guiding principles set out in paragraph 2.6 of last year's EU communication 'The Future Evolution of Social Protection', such an approach is there in Guideline 10: '[...] ensure sound and sustainable public finances. Reforms must ensure that the tax burden arising from public pensions is set at an appropriate level and that other essential public expenditures are not crowded out'.

This is just one of ten excellent guidelines. In a spirit of partnership, we should get these guidelines adopted now. They are not just about costs. Some of them are related to fairness between generations, between different types of workers, etc. But the cost issue can be addressed in the process. All parties can be winners.

Turning to my second suggestion for action: In looking at the options available, the EU states must address the thorny issue of the age of retirement. With ever increasing longevity, I believe the starting-age for pensions must be raised, perhaps to 70, for people retiring towards the middle of the century. With improvements in cancer and heart disease treatment expected over the next ten years, this cannot be dodged. Look at the evidence in our research paper headed 'Healthcast 2010': The available evidence suggest that, following completion of the human genome project, tailored drugs for each of us here today will be available to enable us all to live to 90 and beyond if the cost can be afforded. None of this is in any government projections, or in ours for that matter. Although I believe that the retirement issue should be addressed on current life expectation, future expected improvements make changes in this area vital.

Conclusion

1. Action is required to defuse the pensions time bomb.
2. This action must start now.

Without being prescriptive on specific actions on how benefits should be changed in any individual territory, I have two suggestions:

1. First, set a cost limit for each year until 2050, which must not be exceeded (akin to the Maastricht criteria). Each EU State should then produce an action plan with projections on how they will deliver.
2. Within this plan, my second suggestion is that raising to the start age for pension has to be addressed, possibly to age 70.

The projections and the plan should then be updated every 3 years.

The future of the EU and the Euro in a competitive global economy is dependent on ensuring pension costs do not go too high. Limits must be set and action taken now. Nothing less is acceptable if we want the best for Europe.

Notes

[1]This work is an executive summery of a speech delivered at the one-day conference organised by Friends of Europe with Fortis, Citibank, Deutsche Bank and PricewaterhouseCoopers and in association with Federal Trust and EurActiv.com. The conference was held on the 6th of February, 2001.

Pensions from a Business Perspective[1]

Jos van Niekerk

Managing Director, Unilever Pension Fund, Netherlands

The Need for a Prosperous Europe

The theme of 'Can Europe Pay for its Pensions?' is a very important theme for a multinational company like Unilever, with an important part of its operations in Europe. Unilever employs 255 000 employees worldwide of which about 30 per cent, or 79 000, are employed in European operating companies. Nearly half of Unilever's sales and profits come from Europe.

Therefore, a 'healthy' Europe is very important to us. The successful creation of the single European market is essential for ourselves, as the strategies of Unilever in Europe are based on this European market, which should really function as if it were one big market.

The European Monetary Union delivers a major contribution towards this. Unilever is happy with it during its 2 years of existence. Success of the Euro is clearly inherent. I would like to mention that 12 countries have met the so called convergence criteria in 1999 and 2000, be it that some countries have been engaged in once-off financial transactions to make it easier for them to reach those criteria. However, they have shown that budget deficits could be reduced. A trend towards a further substantial reduction of national debt has started. In addition, another advantage for companies and citizens all over Europe, EMU will help to lower their transaction, and operating, costs.

The ECB has taken up its role and has started its operations. Although there were problems in the beginning, for example when the first president had to be nominated, we are now all used to an ECB in full operation. Its prime goal is price stability in Euroland. Looking at the results so far, we can say that inflation has been fairly low all over Europe. Of course, we cannot look into the future and we do not know what the effect of the increased oil prices or European economic developments will be on inflation. However, we have total confidence that EMU will be helpful in handling this. In addition, we hope that the remaining three EU countries, including the UK, will be able to join EMU soon.

If there is a problem with the Euro, then maybe it is the fact that too many authorities from all European countries are explaining the ECB policies, in slightly different ways, or try to influence them. The financial markets do not seem to appreciate this. Essential is that there is confidence in a real independent ECB.

Fears About Europe's Pensions

When we talk to our pension fund members about the Euro, then people start to ask questions about the purchasing power of their pensions. This is not surprising because the long-term security of the national statutory pension is already an issue in most countries. The replacement of the national currency by the Euro now adds to their uncertainty. What will be the value of the Euro in 30 years from now? Will my pension be worth less because of higher inflation and eroded purchasing power?

There is a fear that the Euro will lead to a so-called 'European pension policy', where those countries with capital funded pension systems will have to subsidise countries with pension systems which are financed on a PAYG basis. Or as some people say, some countries are putting in their assets and others are pouring in their liabilities.

The official answer to the subsidy question is 'no'. There will be no subsidy. Each country will have to pay its own debt and when, for instance, a far too generous pension system in one country would lead to a substantial increase of its national debt, the other EU countries would not participate in that debt.

The pact for stability and growth should give reassurance .The intention is that it supports countries in their decisions on budget discipline, maximal deficits of 3 per cent and sustainable budgets on the longer term.

It is here that I have my doubts on whether the pact is strong enough. In my view, there is ample room for interpretation. Exceeding the limits is tolerated when the situation is 'exceptional' or of 'temporary nature'. Was the Gulf war or the Asian crisis an exceptional event? And what about a major oil price increase? How long do you have to wait until you know it was temporary? Sanctions could be issued. How fast does the system react? Does it take 3 years or 5 years before a possible sanction is effectively paid?

In my view what is important is that there is the political will in each country to avoid increasing deficits and, they have to show this intention. They should have a good insight in the sustainability of the financial situation, of the major revenue – and cost components. Pensions are such a component.

The Long Term Cost Development of Public Pensions

In the Federal Trust report *Can Europe Pay for its Pensions?*, we used the latest data, from 1995, which give a gloomy picture. More recent data have become available in November 2000 in a report drafted by the 'Economic Policy Committee' and discussed by the EcoFin Council. Some countries show better projections than before, like Sweden and Italy, but others, for example Spain, Portugal and the Netherlands show higher increases than before, an extra 6-8 per cent of GDP between now and its peak year in 2030 or 2040. France will also be amongst the countries spending a very large proportion of GDP on pensions.

So there is no reason to sit quiet and wait. Excessive pension cost will most probably lead to higher contributions or taxes, which in the end will have inflationary effects and could easily contaminate the inflation level in other EU countries. ECB would have to raise short-term interest rates and in addition, a higher risk premium in the Euro bondmarkets could materialise. All countries would suffer. In addition, companies in those countries would be faced with higher taxes, higher social security contributions and higher wage costs. Their international competitive position would suffer.

Therefore, I am happy that President Prodi has suggested that EcoFin should issue an annual report on progress made by member states in meeting their pension liabilities. We have seen the first issue of such a report in November last year and you will not be surprised to hear that we will follow closely all further reports, hoping that they will show that the necessary action is taking place.

Pension Funds and Freedom of Investment

For Unilever, attracting and managing the best human resources is one of the major and critical tasks. It lays the foundation for an innovative company and is a major contributor to the long-term success of the company. Offering an attractive remuneration package is of course very important, and pensions form an integral part of this total remuneration concept.

All over the world, Unilever has about 35 pension funds, of which one third is located in Europe.

Total assets of European Unilever pension funds amounts to about nlg 35 billion (about 15.9 billion Euros).

Pension funds are organised on a country by country basis but the establishment of a corporate framework has already achieved a lot of convergence in key issues. Nevertheless Unilever is happy with the initiative of the European Commission which could lead to a single European market for pension funds.

Commissioner Bolkestein knows that pensions are costly and that all possible measures should be taken to make pensions maximally efficient.

Freedom of investment is very important because our experience over a long period indicates that investment in equity makes all the difference in arriving at optimal investment returns.

As I am familiar with the Dutch Unilever pension fund, I would like to give you some figures concerning this fund.

The real return over a 10-year period, ending 1999, amounted to 10.8 per cent per annum; thereby equity outperformed fixed income on average by 8.4 per cent per year over this period.

In addition, over a 20-year period, with a real return of 9.4 per cent per annum, this outperformance of equity over fixed income is high, being in the area of 7 per cent.

A directive with limitations on this point is soon loosing a lot of its attractiveness because for instance a loss of two percentage points in real return can, depending on the parameters of the fund etc, lead to a doubling of pension costs.

In the draft directive, we see that member states have to allow 70 per cent in equity and corporate bond investing. However, they may put a limit indeed at the 70 per cent level and prevent a higher allocation to equity, even when the nature of the liabilities and the financial situation of the fund would allow this. This brings us already far away from full freedom of investment. I really hope that that figure will not change below 70 per cent in the final directive and I hope that individual countries will move away from quantitative limits altogether, such as in the Netherlands and the UK.

Pan-European Pensions

Another important point of the draft directive is that employees can become member of a pension fund across international borders within the EU. This idea of cross border membership is a good idea but it needs to be further developed into a European pension fund. It would help to bring more efficiency in the investment operations and the administration of pension rights of our existing European pension funds. Nevertheless, without a good solution for the fiscal treatment of pension contributions, returns and payments, we see no real possibility to move ahead in Europe quickly. We are glad that Commissioner Bolkestein is aware of the problem and wants to come with a proposal soon. Bilateral tax treaties are no efficient solution in this respect.

The work of the European Federation on Retirement Provision (EFRP) on their concept of a pan-European pooled pension vehicle is very valuable and may help to bring about Institutional Pension Investors on a European scale. It is based on the principle that an established pension fund in one Member State should be able to create sections that are tax approved in other member states. The sections may administer different pension schemes to reflect the difference in the local labour markets, and pension markets, all over Europe. But it is important that they are tax approved. Regulation should take place in its home country. This does imply that pension fund regulators should also be prepared to accept one of the important European principles in the single market: a single licence. They need to understand each others' approach and agree on the new prudential frame work, but avoid the imposition of extra national conditions.

Summary

Coming back to the theme of the conference: Can Europe pay for its pensions? My answer would be: Yes, Europe can do it, but it is essential that:

1. We are able to control the expense of public pensions, that is important and urgent.
2. We have to create European pension institutions and make sure that second pillar pension systems can operate more efficiently throughout Europe, not only in the countries that already have funded pension systems but also in the countries with PAYG systems.

3. We have to opt for efficient saving mechanisms for those pension funds. We would like to eliminate quantitative investment restrictions. Without them we are much better placed to obtain higher returns, which helps Europe to make pensions payable and affordable for the very long-term future.

Note

[1] This paper was delivered on the 6th of February 2001 at the one-day conference on the subject of 'Defusing Europe's Pensions Timebomb'. The conference was organised by Friends of Europe with Fortis, Citibank, Deutsche Bank and PricewaterhouseCoopers and in association with Federal Trust and EurActiv.com.

Draft Report on the proposal for a European Parliament and Council directive on the activities of institutions for occupational retirement provision[1]

Othmar Karas MEP

Committee on Economic and Monetary Affairs

Explanatory Statement

The implementation of measures to guarantee comprehensive retirement provision is one of the key political challenges facing all the EU Member States over the next few years. If appropriate reform measures and a policy for growth and employment are not introduced, the process of demographic change, i.e. constantly increasing life expectancy in conjunction with low birth rates, could call the intergenerational agreement into question and raise fresh doubts as to the scope for financing state pension schemes, which are generally based on the pay-as-you- go system.

With a view to guaranteeing long-term financial stability in old age, in addition to an increase in the retirement age the existing pay-as-you-go system must be supplemented by other forms of funding, i.e. private, long-term saving (third pillar) and funded occupational retirement provision (second pillar).

The Community's task: establishment of an internal market for the second pillar

As a matter of principle, the arrangements under the individual pillars and the related level of pension payments are matters for the Member States. The Community's task is to create the conditions under which these systems can develop as effectively as possible in a single internal market and to take steps to ensure that the varying arrangements do not give rise to long-term obstacles to the freedom of movement of workers and capital and for undertakings active on a cross-border basis.

Although the Community has enacted provisions to govern the cross-border provision of financial services in the sphere of banking, insurance and investment funds, there is no Community legislation under the second pillar. The lack of a single internal market for supplementary occupational retirement provision is detrimental to the financial markets in that funded occupational retirement provision schemes are among the largest institutional investors, whose assets account for more than 20 per cent of the Union's annual GDP.

However, appropriate rules are also vitally needed from the point of view of freedom of movement and the worker flexibility which is so important to today's economy, since workers risk forfeiting their occupational pension entitlements if they change employer. In view of the increasing integration and globalisation of the markets, and above all in a single monetary area, this is a state of affairs which cannot continue.

The urgent need for action has been repeatedly emphasised by the ECOFIN Council and was explicitly confirmed by the Feira European Council in June 2000. In the Action Plan for Financial Services, the establishment of a single prudential framework for funded occupational retirement provision schemes was given the highest priority. The Committee of Wise Men on the regulation of European security markets, chaired by Alexandre Lamfalussy, has repeatedly emphasised the priority which must be attached to this directive and recommended that it should be implemented by 2003 at the latest.

Your rapporteur's objectives

Occupational retirement provision schemes form the link between state social security and private pension saving. The establishment of a prudential framework for the second pillar of retirement provision can thus not be seen in isolation, but instead only against the overall background of social security and with due regard for the social components of pensions. Retirement provision is not simply a financial services product. Security in old age is a significant issue, particularly in connection with the vital task of strengthening of the European social model.

On the basis of these considerations, your rapporteur has set himself four main objectives:

1. Guarantee the protection of beneficiaries and the security of pensions:

Since pension contributions represent a kind of deferred salary payment, protection of the entitlement deriving from these contributions is fundamental, since security in old age has a key role to play in strengthening the European social model. With this aim in view, strict supervisory rules have been laid down and provision made for members of schemes to be provided with comprehensive information.

2. Efficient management and investment on the basis of the prudent person rule:

Institutions should be in a position to invest pension assets efficiently and strike an ideal balance between investment risk and security, on the basis of the prudent person rule. Ultimately, this is advantageous for recipients, since they can expect a higher yield and thus also a higher pension.

3. Clear the way for cross-border activity by institutions:

This represents a vital step towards an internal market in supplementary retirement provision. In this way, investors will be offered a comprehensive range of services and workers will be able to enjoy the benefits of mobility with no risk of forfeiting part of their pension entitlements.

4. Equal treatment for all service providers:

Institutions should be free to seek the services of a more efficient asset manager or custodian established in another Member State. However, this must not give rise to distortions of competition. For that reason, life assurance undertakings should also be subject to this directive in respect of their occupational retirement business.

5. Cost transparency, particularly as regards the biometric risk cover to be offered as an option.

Biometric risk cover: mandatory provision of such an option

Longevity

As a matter of principle, supplementary retirement provision should serve to guarantee financial security until death through the payment of a lifelong pension. There are, therefore, sound arguments in favour of the mandatory payment of the accumulated capital in the form of a lifelong pension. However, this must not necessarily be carried out by the institution for retirement provision itself. The conclusion of a pension contract with another, possibly cheaper, provider is also conceivable. Moreover, there may be cases in which the payment of the capital in a lump sum better serves the purpose of guaranteeing financial security, for example if a person buys a place in a retirement or nursing home. Members of schemes should therefore be granted a degree of freedom, provided that it can be shown that the capital is being used in such a way as to provide lifelong benefits. This can be achieved by stipulating that the payment of a lifelong pension must be offered as a benefit by the institutions for retirement provision, provided that the sponsoring undertaking has not already given a corresponding pledge. For their part, however, members of schemes would not be forced to opt for payment of a lifelong pension. Should members instead opt for a payment of a lump sum, the task of the Member States will be to impose tax penalties for inappropriate use of the capital, as already occurs in some cases. Due account can be taken of the problem of the differing life expectancy of men and women by stipulating that the costs inherent in the payment of the capital in the form of a lifelong pension may not be made contingent on the sex of the person concerned or on an individual health check.

Disability and provision for surviving dependants

Under the first pillar, biometric risks and provision for surviving dependants are normally covered; under the third pillar, the provision of such cover depends on the nature of the individual contract concluded and in the sphere of life assurance it is normally one component of the policy. Given the role of occupational retirement provision as a link between the two pillars, here again the most appropriate approach is to allow a degree of choice. For example, provision for surviving dependants makes little sense in the case of single persons, and a disability pension would appear to be dispensable in cases where other forms of financial provision have been made. Here again, the mandatory availability of an option offers an obvious solution. The requirement that institutions for retirement provision should offer such an option should apply both to provision for disability and for surviving dependants.

In overall terms, the optional availability of biometric risk cover offers the following advantages:

- Members of schemes are forced to think carefully about the financial provision that they have made for their old age and possible shortcomings in that provision.
- In contrast, mandatory biometric risk cover would in practical terms transform supplementary retirement provision products into insurance products and thus hamper competition between the various products.

• The separate identification of the costs involved will guarantee a high degree of transparency. Institutions will thus be unable to justify lower benefits by reference to the provision of biometric risk cover.

• If an institution cannot or may not provide biometric risk cover itself, an external financial service provider (insurance company) may be called in. That firm will calculate its premium partly on the basis of the investment policy pursued by the institution for retirement provision. At the same time, this makes for a high degree for security for members, since, for example, breaches of the prudent person rule would be reflected in higher costs for biometric risk cover. One precondition for this arrangement, however, is that no distinctions should be drawn on the basis of sex and individual risk.

The form of the legal provisions governing investment

The directive requires institutions for supplementary retirement provision, when investing funds, to comply with the prudent person rule. The quantitative rules governing investment which have hitherto obtained in most Member States are replaced by qualitative rules, a move consistent with a general trend in the sphere of financial market regulation and supervision and, increasingly, in the banking sphere. A broadly held prejudice states that the prudent person rule amounts to an untrammelled liberalisation of investment policy, thus laying members of schemes open to a higher degree of risk; in fact, the reverse is true. Pursuant to this rule, funds must be invested in a manner commensurate with the commitments entered into by an institution for supplementary retirement provision, i.e. in particular in a manner commensurate with the age structure of its members. If a majority of those members are at the beginning of their working lives, the investment portfolio should consist largely of shares, since, temporary fluctuations not withstanding, in the long term shares offer a substantially better return than fixed-rate securities. In contrast, an institution most of whose members have already reached pensionable age might already be in breach of the prudent person rule if shares made up 10 per cent of its portfolio.

At the same time, the flexibility which goes hand in hand with the prudent person rule clears the way for more effective portfolio diversification and, in turn, a lower degree of investment risk than would be the case under strict, quantitative rules. Greater responsibility will be placed on the shoulders of the supervisory authorities, since they will be required to assess in individual cases whether the investment policy pursued by an institution is consistent with the principle of prudence in terms of security, quality, liquidity and efficiency.

However, the directive must also take account of differing investment mentalities in the individual Member States and the lack of experience which the relevant national authorities have with a qualitative approach to the supervision of institutions for supplementary retirement provision. For this reason, the directive offers Member States the possibility of retaining quantitative rules, subject to certain restrictions. In this connection, your rapporteur advocates a time-limit: Member States should indeed be given the option of retaining quantitative restrictions, but this option should apply only for an appropriate period, not exceeding ten years, in which time a Member State's 'supervisory culture and methods' can be brought into line with the qualitative approach.

Equal treatment for all providers under the second pillar

One of the main aims of the directive is to establish equal conditions of competition for all participants in the market under the second pillar. The introduction of an option on the basis of which the occupational retirement provision business of insurance undertakings can be brought within the scope of this directive is consistent with this approach, since insurance undertakings are active in the market under the second pillar, in particular through group and direct insurance policies, but are subject to the provisions of the third life assurance directive in respect of supervision and investment. However, your rapporteur takes the view that the decision on whether to introduce such an option should not be left to the Member States, since this might once again give rise to differing conditions of competition, among the undertakings concerned and under the second pillar, from one Member State to another. With a view to ruling out such disparities, the choice of framework should be left to the undertakings themselves.

However, the provision in the Commission text requiring insurance undertakings wishing to operate under the second pillar to create a separate legal entity does not appear to be justified, since the undertakings concerned must be granted a degree of flexibility to organise their business activities. It is not desirable that a compulsory legal form should be laid down, since the most suitable solution generally depends on conditions on the market in question, particularly in terms of tax and the relevant provisions of social and labour law.

Insurance undertakings should have the choice of setting up a separate legal entity or of managing that business by establishing a separate clearing system. The establishment of a separate clearing system could make sense, because the establishment of a separate legal entity generates additional, particularly administrative, costs and might involve unnecessary red tape. Nevertheless, provision would have to be made for a clear separation of the pension-related assets and separate accounts.

Your rapporteur proposes differing arrangements for the application of the directive in the two cases. Under the first arrangement, the establishment of a separate legal entity for retirement provision business under the second pillar, the new institutions would be subject to the full provisions of this directive. In the event of the establishment of a separate clearing system, occupational retirement provision business would be subject only to the provisions of this directive governing supervision and investment. In order to guarantee the separation of the assets relating to occupational retirement provision business, however, the competent authorities in each Member State would have to be given the task of monitoring that strict separation as part of their supervisory role.

Further measures fundamental to the establishment of an internal market

The proposal for a directive, and, in particular, the provisions stipulating mutual recognition of prudential standards, represents an important first step towards the establishment of an internal market for supplementary retirement provision. On its own, however, it will not be enough. Further measures must follow since the portability of pensions and mobility within the European Union will only become a reality once the Member States have reached agreement on uniform tax principles. Although the amount of taxation, as one aspect of income tax arrangements, is a matter for the Member States, a transition to deferred taxation (EET system) would be desirable in order to prevent the double taxation or non-taxation of contributions and benefits.

The elimination of the discriminatory tax practices employed by many Member States vis-à-vis foreign service providers and the pension contributions paid by nationals of other EU Member States, practices which can be equated with a compartmentalisation of the pension market, is a further precondition, not least because non-discrimination is one of the fundamental principles underlying the internal market. The Member States should honour their undertakings and do away with these discriminatory practices, which represent a clear breach of the principles of freedom of movement for workers and non-discrimination laid down in the EC Treaty and in the established case law of the CJEC, as soon as possible. This would clear the way for development of a functioning internal market in supplementary pensions, without additional legislation being required at European level.

---

[1] Co-decision procedure (first reading), majority of the votes cast. This draft report was presented to the Committee on Economic and Monetary Affairs on the 9th of March 2001.

The EU dimension for Pension Reform[1]

Kees Van Rees,

Chairman,
European Federation for
Retirement Provision (EFRP)

The Federal Trust ought to be complemented for their initiative to prepare a second report on EU pension issues [chaper 1 of present volume]. The title of the present report is much less threatening than the 1995 *The Pension Time Bomb in Europe*. The report mentions substantial changes in Europe and postulates that 'EU countries will be able to meet their future pension liabilities within the limits of the Maastricht Treaty and the Growth and Stability pact'. It brings our attention to favourable developments. Unfortunately, this conclusion is hardly backed up by an analysis of the report. For example, page 11 tells us that 'projections of future public spending on pensions in Europe do not show a reassuring picture,' and page 13 indicates that without change, pension contributions will rise from the current figure of 13.76 per cent to 20.5 per cent in 2020 and around 26 per cent in 2030. This is hardly a review of reassuring developments.

Recent Pensions Reforms in the EU

The report rightly points to very encouraging reforms in Sweden and Ireland. It is a pity that Sweden and Ireland have populations that account for no more than 3.36 per cent of the EU population. In contrast, policy developments in the larger countries are stalling. Some 300 kilometres South of Brussels a pension war is in progress. There is much talk East of the Rhine, but no substantial agreement on measures as yet. South of the Alps people still retire in their early fifties: a 'dolce far niente'! The real problem is supposed to accelerate by the year 2010, when the baby boomers officially retire; but that is two terms of Parliament away.

So, the track record of pension reform in the EU member states is not encouraging. In this climate of change it should not surprise us to find that the progress within the EU respecting pension reform is rather dismal. In the last decade nothing of real significance has been legislated, despite courageous initiatives from the EU Commission. The EU Court of Justice has pronounced on Equal Treatment. Issues of direct and indirect discrimination have excited politicians everywhere, leading to all sorts of retrospective changes for pension funds. But where does this leave the first pillar? For years basic inequalities have persisted.

Scope for Further Reforms

What can the EU do in an environment where Member States differ ideologically on the way ahead? What can the EU do in a climate where the governments of Member States count present and future votes for critical and criticised measures, which will have a real impact in 10 years time? With due respect to Mr Bolkestein,[2] there is no 'Schuman' on pensions in sight, who with foresight and authority will be able to promote and implement the necessary policies. For the time being the motto is 'muddle through, never mind the long-term consequences.'

Meanwhile, the EU can make some material contributions. Firstly, they should be able to create a system of independent and honest accounting in the area of pensions. These accounts ought to have a common base set of definitions. Thereafter, the EU Commission ought to promote independent assessments and audits. Hence, no TEULADE type reports, please.

Secondly, the EU Commission ought to persevere in promoting its proposals for a directive on supplementary pensions. EFRP has submitted its comments. Generally speaking, we want a strengthening of the proposals for freedom of investment. There should be no further watering down, no exceptions to the basic rules. We need a collective approach, which would be cheaper in all respects. Content should be left to employers and employees, who are often represented by social partners. The cross-border aspect ought to be central to the proposal, although without it any sensible Member State could take all of the necessary measures.

Cross-Border Pensions and Taxation

Cross-border pensions are seriously hampered by the diversity of taxation arrangements for pensions in Member States. EFRP has prepared a proposal on a European Institution for Occupational Retirement Provision that goes a long way towards tackling the tax differences on pensions in cross-border traffic. I urge the Commission to give this proposal a place in its overall taxation proposals.

A lack of action on this issue costs European industry sizeable amounts of money annually.

A bold step on taxation would be the implementation of the EET principle on pensions. I understand that Commissioner Bolkestein has indicated his long-term support on this matter, but what about the European Parliament? Member States are gradually encountering budget surpluses. Now is the right time to invest some of this money on EET principle.

The Euro will make unexplained or unexplainable differences visible. Hopefully this will stimulate European citizens to ask some penetrating questions on the issue of pensions. By 2002, it will also become very clear that it is hard to conduct an effective monetary and economic policy, while excluding some alignment of fiscal and social security policies. I draw some hope from this fact, that even on pensions there is more than a glimmer of light at the end of the tunnel.

Summary

I am much less hopeful with respect to the question *Can Europe Pay for its Pensions?* than the Federal Trust Report. A lot of reforms still need to be made. At EU level it will have taken almost a generation of pensioners since the first initiative on pension funds in 1989 to the current proposal for a directive becoming full operational.

Honest accounting and auditing of pension data and issues ought to be pursued at EU level, and cross-border mobility on pensions requires some bold steps on the part of EU member States. The introduction of the Euro may well force policy makers to act on social security, which is closely linked to supplementary pensions and taxation. However, the question still remains: 'Do we need a real crisis before EU leaders act?'

Notes

[1] This is an executive summary from a speech delivered to the Friends of Europe conference in Brussles on the 6th of February.

[2] See chapter 6 for Frits Bolkestein's *Closing Remarks for the Friends of Europe Conference.*

Closing Remarks for the *Friends of Europe* Conference[1]

Frits Bolkestein

European Commissioner for the Internal Market

It is easy to get pessimistic about the pensions timebomb, for at least three reasons:

1. The ratio of workers to pensioners will decline from 4 to 1 to less than 2 to 1 by 2040;
2. If unfunded pension liabilities were budgetised, in some Member States this would represent a debt of over 200 per cent of GDP;
3. Even with the current reform in place for public pension schemes, spending will increase by between 3 per cent and 5 per cent of GDP in most countries.

These figures are more than explicit, and could become even worse if, for example, there were a significant increase in life expectancy.

Let me be clear: the primary responsibility for meeting this pensions challenge lies with the Member States. They have to make tough political decisions on reform of the public pension: how much workers must pay in contributions, how long will they have to contribute, how much pension they will get.

Clearly the solutions to the impending problem – pay more, work longer, get less – is not an easy message to sell. Member States also must decide on the role to be played by funded pension schemes – either linked to employment or on an individual basis – and what tax incentives they will give to stimulate such funding.

My remarks will highlight what I believe is the added value that the Union can bring to Member States pensions policies and reforms. Community action can help underpin the reforms that Member States are now making to defuse this timebomb. These reforms do not yet eliminate all our concerns over ageing, but start a process to alleviate the negative scenario that is approaching.

I will focus my remarks on the Commission's initiatives in the field of ageing and its implications for pensions and then turn to those initiatives which are linked with the internal market and taxation and fall more directly under my responsibility within the Commission.

Commission initiatives to tackle the implications of ageing

The Commission is tackling the implications of ageing on both the economic and the social fronts. These policies form a coherent and co-ordinated approach. They will make a valuable contribution towards finding effective solutions.

Economic Measures

The ability to pay pensions requires sound and sustainable public finances; which in turn is needed for the success of EMU and the Euro; which in turn sets the right economic environment for investment, growth and job creation; which in turn creates the ability to pay pensions. This is a virtuous circle.

However, pensions payments could easily turn into a vicious circle. If pension spending were not reformed, but led to higher deficits, some countries would not respect their obligations under the growth and stability pact; which in turn could lead to inflationary pressures; which would result in the ECB having to set higher interest rates with negative impact not only on investment, but also on growth and employment, which are the basis of sustainable pension systems.

This is the reasoning behind the Commission's work – together with the Economic Policy Committee – on the impact of ageing populations and public pension systems. The Commission is encouraging Member States to set in place a comprehensive reform process to address these challenges, including:

- Running down public debt at a faster pace so as to lower the interest burden and offset increased pension spending;
- Raising employment rates, especially of older workers and women, so as to reduce the ratio of dependants to active workers;
- Proceeding with further reforms of public pension systems, including moves towards greater reliance on funding.

The Commission and the Council will be making a joint report to the Stockholm summit in March on the best way to make progress on these issues.

Social Measures

The Commission is also active on the social front. The Lisbon Council asked for a study of social protection from a long-term point of view, paying particular attention to pensions. In October 2000 the Commission issued a Communication on safe and sustainable pensions.[2]

This marries well with work on the economic front. One particular feature I should like to highlight is the need to change policies that currently seem to discourage older workers from participating in the labour market. Pension systems tend to offer strong incentives for early withdrawal from the labour market. In addition, older workers' job skills are often outdated. As a result, fewer than a quarter of people aged 60-64 are in employment! Policies must be found to reverse this trend. We need these older workers to be economically active, not dependent on a shrinking number of younger workers.

Reforms Related to Funded Pensions and Taxation

Let me now turn to the two initiatives for which I am more directly responsible – funded pensions and taxation. It is clear from what I have said concerning reforms already being carried out that there will be greater reliance put on funded pensions as part of the solution for sustainability:

- Some Member States already have large well developed funds;
- In some Member States these funds are growing rapidly, albeit from a small base;
- Some Member States, notably Germany, are involved in an active political debate on the role of such funds.

Whatever role they play, it is important that pensions funds operate as efficiently and safely as possible. I believe that the Commission's proposals in this area, with the proposed directive on the supervision of pension funds adopted on 11 October 2000, can enhance both their efficiency and their safety. But first let me explain the objectives of the directive:

- Obviously we want security of pensions.
- Less obviously, and sometimes without due prominence, is the affordability of these pensions. A secure pension fund that is unaffordable for the majority of workers, or gives too small a pension in relation to the contributions is as bad news as lack of security.

- Finally, by having common prudential standards, we can also permit cross-border membership. Today, companies have to operate separate pension funds in every Member State in which they employ workers. By pooling these pension funds they could achieve very significant cost savings. It should also be much easier for staff of these companies to move from one subsidiary to another.

In order to meet these objectives, the Directive provides a full prudential framework, which is also needed to provide the mutual recognition between Member States – the basis of cross-border membership.

But the prudential framework also promotes affordability. I know that there has been some concern in Member States with large funds. They fear that the efficiency of their funds could be harmed if a deal is struck in Council and Parliament that would tighten prudential rules and impose certain investment strategies that would lead to lower returns to accommodate those Member States who do not have large funds yet. Let me be clear. The 'prudent expert' principle has operated successfully for decades and it would be unwise to start telling the trustees and social partners who run pension funds in the interests of workers and pensioners how they should do their job.

Let me give you some numbers to illustrate this issue – how small changes in returns can make a huge difference:

- If pension funds were all in bonds, then the cost of an average pension would be 15 per cent of salary.
- If pension funds were all in shares, then the cost of pensions would be 5 per cent of salary.

It is up to those managing a pension fund to decide which combination of bonds and shares is best, taking into account the age structure of members. No rules should be imposed that unjustifiably prevent efficient investment policies: otherwise costs spiral and pension fund managers will not be able to serve the best interests of their members.

To look at it another way, a 0.5 per cent increase in administrative costs or reduction in return on assets means a 20 per cent reduction in final pension. Again I conclude that we should avoid unnecessary rules or bureaucracy, which would increase administrative or running costs of pension funds, which would in turn mean less pensions.

I believe that the Commission's proposal is a good one to achieve our aims. If adopted it will add value to national policies. By allowing pension funds to take full advantage of the Euro, the Single Market and cross-border membership, it will allow them to operate more efficiently. And, as the figures I quoted demonstrate, small efficiency gains can have a huge impact on costs and pensions.

Further Debate on Social Aspects

I am aware of the concerns that prevail in some circles about the lack of consideration given to the social aspects of pension reforms. Let me be clear on this point: the social and redistributive implications of the reform of our pension systems are vitally important to the maintenance of the European social model and of ensuring a decent standard of living for all retired people. A debate on these issues must take place.

It must be discussed in the appropriate circles, including with the social partners. However, the Commission's proposal has neither the ambition nor the objective to deal with these wider issues. It is much more modest but nevertheless important. Its objective is to make existing or future pension funds safer and more cost effective as well as improve the portability of pensions.

It will be a major challenge in Council and Parliament to find ways to accommodate the huge variety of situations concerning pension funds in the different Member States. But we cannot do this at the cost of funds operating efficiently and securely.

Providing for Cross-Border Occupational Pensions

In Council, the Swedish Presidency has had two meetings of experts. They will continue to work intensively. I understand that their aim is to have an orientation debate with Finance Ministers in May to raise and try to unblock any key issues outstanding. But the Presidency would also like to broaden the debate to the taxation issues related to pensions.

The proposed Pension Fund Directive does not deal with the tax obstacles to the cross-border provision of occupational pensions. In many instances these tax obstacles prohibit migrant workers from remaining in their pension scheme in their State of origin, and in many instances workers in one Member State cannot join a pension scheme operated by a pension provider in another Member State. In other words, these tax obstacles stand in the way of a fully functioning Single Market for occupational pensions.

The Commission is preparing a Communication to address these issues, which should be published in March 2001. The main point will be the tax obstacles to the cross-border provision of occupational pensions I just mentioned.

The initiative will also contain proposals to improve the exchange of information on cross-border pensions between Member States and it will explore ways of dealing with the existing diversity of Member States' pension taxation systems.

Conclusion

This conference intervenes at a moment when we are becoming more confident about our ability to meet the challenge of ageing, one of the Swedish Presidency's priorities. It is, after all, paradoxical that rising life expectancy – one of the greatest achievements of the last century – is being presented as the scourge of the new century.

We are now starting to look for solutions and the four inter-connected initiatives that I described are the contribution of the Commission. Let us work together to make them succeed.

Notes

[1] Conference held on the 6th of February, 2001.

[2] Communication from the Commission: *The Future Evolution of Social Protection from a Long-Term Point of View: Safe and Sustainable Pensions* COM (2000)622 11.10.2000 IP/00/1143.

Proposal for a Directive of the European Parliament and of the Council on the activities of institutions for occupational retirement provision

Commission of the European Communities

EXPLANATORY MEMORANDUM

The Lisbon European Council placed strong emphasis on the need to integrate financial services and markets within the Union. A single financial market will be a key factor in promoting the competitiveness of the European economy, the development of the new economy and social cohesion. That is why the Heads of State and Government called for the Financial Services Action Plan to be implemented by 2005. In its conclusions, the Presidency stresses that priority must be given to removing the remaining barriers to investment in the field of pension funds.

Such funds play a major role in promoting social cohesion in many Member States and in financing Europe's economy. In view of the ageing of the Union's population, it is vital to ensure that they can operate with maximum security and efficiency.

The security of pensions is of prime importance: the rights of future pensioners must be protected by strict prudential standards. However, attention must also be paid to the cost of pensions. If pension benefits are too expensive given low returns or excessive administrative constraints, everyone will lose out. The competitiveness of firms will be affected, it will be more difficult for the pension schemes to break even and pensioners might end up receiving smaller benefits.

Consequently, this proposal for a Directive on institutions for occupational retirement provision is designed to strike the best possible balance between security and affordability.

1. GENERAL COMMENTS

1.1. The need for a Community legal framework covering institutions for occupational retirement provision

(a) Institutions for occupational retirement provision and their social and economic importance.

There are three main categories of pension schemes in the Member States: social security schemes, individual schemes, which generally take the form of contracts or products taken out with life-assurance companies, and occupational schemes. The general organisation and financing of these schemes is the responsibility of the Member States.

Occupational schemes generally involve employer and employees paying into a savings scheme, out of which retirement benefits will be paid to these same employees. Such schemes may be set up within the company itself or may use the services of a separate financial institution (e.g. pension fund, 'Pensionskassen' or investment fund) which receives the contributions, invests them and pays out the retirement benefits.

Such institutions, which will here be referred to as 'institutions for occupational retirement provision' (IORPs), play a major role in retirement and social protection systems in a number of Member States. It is estimated that close on 25 per cent of the Union's active population is covered by an occupational pension scheme. The proportion can be higher than 80 per cent in some countries, such as the Netherlands or Denmark, while relatively low in others. The share of occupational pensions in total pensions is around 10 per cent.

The value of the assets held by these institutions exceeds EUR 2,000 billion, i.e. it is equivalent to about 25 per cent of the Union's GDP (a little more than 45 per cent for the assets of insurance companies). They thus play, along with the other financial institutions, a key role in financing Europe's economy and in the operation of the Union's capital markets.

IORPs are also characterised by the very long-term nature of their activities, both in terms of commitment of the sponsoring undertaking and in terms of investment. They invest for several decades and, since contributions paid to an IORP can in general not be withdrawn before the age of retirement, they ought to have a very good idea of what their cash requirements will be. This allows them, if they consider it appropriate in the light of the nature and duration of the liabilities, to invest significantly in relatively non-liquid assets such as shares, including those issued by small businesses, or even unlisted securities. IORPs can thus contribute to risk capital development in accordance with the guidelines set out in the Risk Capital Action Plan[1], which was endorsed by the Cardiff European Council. With a view to improving the diversification of their investment portfolios, they can also invest substantially in foreign securities. 75 per cent of the assets of UK pension funds in 1998, for example, were in shares. A third of these shares were foreign.

Institutions for occupational retirement provision thus play a major role in national social protection systems, in the financing of the Union's economy and in the integration of its capital markets. There is good reason to think that, in the decades to come, they will remain at the centre of economic and social change in the Union. Demographic developments (extension of life expectancy and fall in birth rates) are prompting the growth of pension savings. The latter can help to reduce public expenditure while also guaranteeing a high level of retirement benefits and thus the preservation of the European social model. IORPs are investing more in shares, considered more advantageous in the long term. In doing so, they contribute to the increase of the stock market capitalisation of the Member States, which is still about half that of the United States. Lastly, it may be desired by sponsoring undertakings and beneficiaries that IORPs provide pension services across Europe.

These developments mean that an appropriate Community framework must be set in place.

(b) The absence of a Community framework and the negative consequences of this gap

The European Union now has detailed prudential rules for credit institutions, insurance companies and undertakings for collective investment in transferable securities (UCITS). These rules provide security for consumers and investors. A proposal for a Directive relating to the freedom of management and investment of funds held by institutions for retirement provision[2] had to be withdrawn by the Commission in 1994 since no satisfactory agreement could be found in the Council. To date, the activities of IORPs have not been subject to any specific Community rules. This gap has several negative consequences.

- **Investment.** There is no agreement within the Community on how IORPs can use the single market and the Euro to optimise their investments in financial markets. The rules to which they must adhere vary greatly from one Member State to another. The possibility cannot be ruled out that some of these rules go beyond what is necessary to ensure the IORPs' prudential soundness. If so, this could hinder the application of the principle of the free movement of capital and damage the IORPs' returns. Between 1984 and 1998, average annual real return on investments by IORPs was around 6 per cent in the Member States with strict quantitative investment rules and more than 10 per cent in Member States with rules that give managers more freedom. Lower returns mean lower pay-outs or higher contributions. The indirect cost of labour rises, as does the cost of financing retirement systems. Investment policy in the field of supplementary pensions depends on the pension product and the contractual obligation of the pension provider. By limiting opportunities for diversification of assets, rules that are too restrictive might also complicate risk management and reduce the security of investment portfolios. Excessive restrictions on shares, which are usually less volatile than government bonds in the long term given their link to economic and productivity growth, can have a negative impact in this regard. It is therefore vital that an agreement be reached on investment rules that are suited to the more extensive and more liquid capital market that is the result of economic and monetary union.

• **Allocation of savings.** IORPs have a key role to play in the integration, efficiency and liquidity of these markets. As very long-term investors, they are ideally placed to assist the financing of private initiatives. While the security and profitability of investment portfolios is a priority objective, a Community framework can also ensure that the IORPs participate in the efficient allocation of savings in the Union.

• **Managing and custody of assets.** IORPs may find themselves obliged to use only the services of custodians or asset managers established in the same Member State as themselves. However, if IORPs are to be given the means of improving their investment policy, they must be able to choose their managers freely. Investment in a given sector or region may require the services or advice of a specialised manager, who may not necessarily be based in the same Member State as the IORP. Furthermore, if competition between managers and between custodians were increased, this might help to cut management costs and make management more efficient. There ought to be specific community rules giving IORPs the right to use the services of managers duly authorised under the investment services Directive, the Directive on credit institutions and the third life-assurance Directive[3]. This right should be extended to management companies in accordance with a proposal for a Directive on UCITS[4] currently being discussed by Council and Parliament.

• **Cross-border activities.** In the absence of proper coordination at Community level, IORPs are the only major financial institutions unable to provide their services in a Member State other than their own on the same conditions as banks, insurance companies and investment firms. It has been calculated that, for a pan-European company, the cost of setting up separate occupational systems in each Member State is about EUR 40 million per year. Allowing IORPs to manage schemes for companies established in another Member State would result in economies of scale of several types: more efficient investment policies as a result of asset pooling, simplification of administration and compliance with the prudential and reporting rules of a single supervisory authority. Furthermore, labour mobility would become easier: workers could more easily take up a job in another Member State if they could remain members of the same IORP, as is foreseen, for posted workers under the terms of Title II of Regulation (EEC) No 1408/71, in Directive 98/49/EC on safeguarding the supplementary pension rights of employed and self-employed persons moving within the Community; multinationals would come up against fewer obstacles to moving their employees from one Member State to another.

• **Growth of the IORPs.** Promoting occupational retirement savings can help to balance the financing of pension systems and put state schemes on a sounder financial footing. This decision is for the Member States to take and requires in particular that appropriate tax incentives be set in place. The existence of a legal framework containing European prudential standards and allowing cross-border management of occupational schemes would however be more conducive to the growth of IORPs than are the partitioning of markets and the regulatory patchwork that prevail today.

(c) The results of the consultation process launched by the Commission and the Financial Services Action Plan

The European Parliament, Economic and Social Committee and the financial services sector have been pressing for several years for the establishment of a European framework for IORPs. This is quite clear from the consultation process and the proposals made by the Commission in a Green Paper 5 in 1997[5] and a Communication[6] in 1999. On 13 April 2000, the European Parliament adopted a Resolution[7] which welcomes the Commission's intention to propose a Directive on supplementary pensions.

Several Member States also expressed their support, in their responses to the 1997 Green Paper, for the adoption of a directive. Furthermore, the Member States, at the Cologne European Council in June 1999, endorsed the Financial Services Action Plan[8] proposed by the Commission in May 1999. One of the strategic objectives of this Plan consists in establishing a genuine single market for wholesale financial transactions. The adoption of legislative provisions on investments by IORPs is presented in the Plan as a prerequisite to attaining this objective.

The proposed Directive lays down prudential rules designed to ensure that occupational pension transactions attain a high level of security and efficiency. These rules also allow mutual recognition of the supervisory systems of the Member States, a prerequisite for cross-border management of occupational schemes.

1.2. The objectives of the proposal

(a) Secure and efficient investment

The proposed Directive stresses a qualitative approach to investment rules. Investment portfolio management should preferably comply with principles (security, quality, liquidity, return, diversification) and not uniform quantitative requirements. In this way, each IORP can apply the principles listed according to the nature and duration of its liabilities. This will guarantee security and efficiency. In Member States which take this approach, the returns on investments by IORPs are usually higher than those in Member States with a more quantitative approach.

Discussions so far have tended to indicate that some Member States would nevertheless prefer to continue to apply certain quantitative rules to IORPs established on their territory. This is essentially because supervisory methods used in those Member States are closely linked to the application of quantitative rules. The proposed Directive takes their wishes into account. However, it does propose that three types of investment should not be restricted excessively: shares, securities denominated in a non-matching currency, and risk capital. Where IORPs have very long term liabilities and face relatively low liquidity risks, they should be given the possibility to invest significantly in securities that are not very liquid and are denominated in a different currency from that in which the liability is denominated.

(b) Free choice of asset managers and custodians

As indicated above, IORPs should be guaranteed the right to use the services of any duly authorised manager or custodian within the Union.

(c) Level playing-field between all service providers

Life-assurance companies operate on the market for occupational pensions via group contracts. Such companies are regulated at Community level by the life-assurance Directives. Prudential rules for other IORPs should therefore be determined in such a way as not to introduce distortions of competition. The establishment of a real prudential framework should in general avoid such distortions. In addition, where the services of IORPs resemble those offered in group contracts – for example, where the IORP offers a financial guarantee – similar rules to those set out in the life-assurance Directives are suggested for own capital requirements. If a Member State considers that greater consistency must be implemented in the prudential treatment of IORPs and life-assurance companies, it should be able to apply certain prudential provisions of this Directive to the occupational pension business of life-assurance companies. This option is given to Member States.

(d) Cross-border activities

By harmonising certain basic prudential rules, establishing mutual recognition of national prudential systems and proposing a system of notification and cooperation between competent authorities, this Directive removes all prudential barriers to cross-border management of IORP pension schemes. If cross-border activities is to become a reality, a certain degree of tax coordination between Member States will also be necessary. It should in particular be possible for companies and employees to obtain tax relief on contributions that are paid into a IORP established in another Member State. In other words, contributions to domestic IORP's and to IORP's established in other Member States should be treated with neutrality. This aspect is not dealt with here but will be the subject of a separate proposal by the Commission.

Furthermore, the Directive stipulates that cross-border management must comply with social and labour legislation in the country of the company within which the scheme is established. Schemes must be run in conformity with national provisions, regardless of where the IORP is located.

(e) Protection of beneficiaries

Cross-border activities require a certain level of prudential harmonisation. Before allowing an IORP established in another Member State to manage pension schemes on its territory, each Member State must ensure that the IORP in question is regulated and supervised in such a way that the rights of beneficiaries are given appropriate protection. This proposal therefore includes a set of basic prudential rules (competence and good repute of managers, conditions for access to the activity, information provided to members and beneficiaries, regulatory own funds, investment rules), together with rules on IORP liabilities including technical provisions.

Generally speaking, affording the best protection to future pensioners is the Commission's primary objective. Contributions paid to an IORP are a form of deferred salary. The rights acquired by the payment of these contributions determine the standard of living of those concerned. Protecting these rights is thus at the very heart of the wider objective of strengthening the European social model.

(f) The single market for financial services

Coordinating investment and management rules applicable to IORPs is one of the components of the Financial Services Action Plan. With a major gap in current Community legislation on financial services filled, a decisive step will have been taken in the direction of a single market for financial services capable of fully promoting growth and employment.

(g) The single market for supplementary pensions

The adoption of this Directive would also be a step towards allowing supplementary pension provision to be organised at the level of the Single Market. Investors would have access to a wider choice of service providers and workers could move around without running the risk of losing part of their pension rights. This would contribute to economic and social progress, but will require greater coordination of the tax, social and labour legislation of the Member States.

1.3. The approach taken

(a) Avoiding any interference in the organisation of pension systems in the Member States

The general organisation of pension schemes, the choice of financing mechanisms and the precise arrangements for the operation of IORPs fall within the competence of the Member States as long as Treaty rules are respected. This prerogative is not compromised by the current proposal.

(b) Ensuring consistency with Community financial services legislation

The approach taken in preparing this proposal was institution-based, in accordance with the approach taken in all other Community legislation adopted in the financial services field. Such an approach is also suited to the cross-border activity mechanisms that, it is hoped, will be set in place. None the less, the prudential rules are inseparable from the benefits promised by the IORPs (defined benefits or contributions, possible cover of biometric risks). The proposed Directive therefore includes, where necessary, rules that are differentiated according to the type of scheme.

(c) Establishing a coherent scope

The Directive covers all IORPs which operate on a funded basis and are outside the social security systems. This ensures that, in a field where disparities between countries are very wide by comparison with other financial activities, the scope of the Directive is relatively coherent.

Briefly, any institution that receives contributions and invests them with the sole purpose of paying out retirement benefits is considered to be an IORP. It is vital that the assets held by IORPs cannot be used for any purpose other than the payment of capital or an annuity at retirement age. In other words, the rights acquired cannot be 'surrendered' before the age of retirement, otherwise the scheme does not constitute a pension scheme but a savings product.

The Directive does not stipulate that benefits must be paid out in the form of an annuity or that precise biometric risks need to be covered by the institution. When discussing the Communication on supplementary pensions, the Parliament focused a great deal on this specific issue and finally came to the conclusion that longevity risks needed to be insured.

From the point of view of the Commission, it is desirable that the precise arrangements for the payment of benefits, which are often dependent on national tax, labour and social law, be decided inside the Member States. Moreover, prudential standards need to be established which apply to all occupational pension products. Companies and investors would gain nothing from certain products (in this case defined contribution schemes which provide only for the payment of capital without covering biometrical risks) being excluded from all European legislation. Therefore, all types of IORP schemes are covered in this Directive, even if the Commission considers that cover for longevity risks in particular is an important aspect of the fight against poverty and insecurity among elderly people.

The few IORPs which operate on a pay-as-you-go basis are not covered by the proposed Directive. This does not pose any problems given the main policy objectives of the proposal. The efficiency of financial investments and the use of managers from other Member States are not issues for these institutions, which use contributions to finance pay-outs directly. Member States or competent institutions cope with mismatches between contributions and benefits through additional contributions or tax revenues.

Firms which establish book reserves in order to provide retirement benefits to their employees are also not covered by this Directive. The use of book reserves, which is permitted in a limited number of Member States only, leaves firms completely free to decide how to use the assets covering their liabilities. Guaranteeing freedom of investment and management by means of a Directive therefore does not seem necessary here. Moreover, a guarantee or insolvency insurance fund generally replaces any prudential rules.

Lastly, consultations so far have shown that neither IORPs operating on a pay-as-you-go basis nor firms which establish book reserves wish to benefit from cross-border activities, at least by using these types of schemes.

(d) Taking account of national diversity while ensuring a high level of protection

IORPs operate very differently from one Member State to another. In some Member States, they resemble life-assurance companies. In others, they are more like investment funds. The Directive proposed takes account of these differences, which are often linked to tax and social security legislation in the Member States. It cannot seek to harmonise in detail the conditions under which IORPs operate.

Their diversity also necessarily restricts the degree of prudential harmonisation that can be attained by this initial proposal for a Directive. However, an extremely rigorous approach has been adopted for the most crucial prudential aspects (financing liabilities, diversification of assets, information to be provided to the supervisory authorities, members and beneficiaries). This should enable the fundamental objective of a high level of protection for the rights of present and future pensioners to be attained and to permit mutual recognition.

2. DESCRIPTION OF ARTICLES

Article 2 – Scope

• This proposal is concerned with institutions operating occupational pension schemes. These are private schemes, usually seen as supplementing statutory social security schemes. It is essential to preserve a clear distinction between statutory social security and private/supplementary schemes. This proposal is therefore not concerned with social security schemes which are covered by the term 'legislation' as defined by Article 1 of Regulation (EEC) No 1408/71 or in respect of which a Member State has made a declaration under that Article.

• Life-insurance companies, Undertakings for Collective Investment in Transferable Securities (UCITS), credit institutions and institutions covered by the Investment Service Directive already benefit from a Single Market framework. It does not seem to be necessary to include them in this new Directive, even though they might be capable of providing occupational pension services.

• In Germany, institutions known as 'Unterstützungskassen' are one of the practicable forms of financing occupational pensions. Unterstützungskassen are support funds and similar to IORPs in that the accumulation of assets is external. The difference between these funds and IORPs is that no legal right to benefits of a certain amount is established for members. For tax reasons Unterstützungskassen are generally underfunded. The employer can redeem the assets at any time and not necessarily meet its obligation for payments. A statutory insolvency insurance is compulsory in order to protect the interests of the members adequately. Thus Unterstützungskassen are not subject to any prudential supervision. Given these characteristics, such funds cannot be compared to IORPs in other Member States covered by this Directive and are therefore excluded.

• Firms which establish book reserves in order to provide retirement benefits to their employees are also not covered by this Directive. The use of book reserves, which is permitted in a limited number of Member States only, leaves firms completely free to decide how to use the assets covering their liabilities. Guaranteeing freedom of investment and management by means of a directive therefore does not seem necessary here. Moreover, a guarantee or insolvency insurance fund generally replaces any prudential rules.

• The few IORPs which operate on a pay-as-you-go basis are also not covered by the proposed Directive. The efficiency of financial investments and the use of managers from other Member States are not issues for these institutions, which use contributions to finance pay-outs directly. Member States or competent institutions cope with mismatches between contributions and benefits through additional contributions or tax revenues.

Article 3 – Application to institutions operating social security schemes

In at least one Member State, IORPs have to operate two types of schemes: voluntary employment related pension schemes (considered as supplementing social security) and compulsory employment related pension schemes (considered as social security). It is proposed to include these institutions for the voluntary/ supplementary part of their activity.

Article 4 – Optional application to institutions covered by Directive 79/267/EEC

As already mentioned as regards Article 2, it does not seem necessary to include life-insurance companies, Undertakings for Collective Investment in Transferable Securities (UCITS), credit institutions and institutions covered by the Investment Service Directive in this Directive. However, any inequality of treatment resulting from separate prudential frameworks must be avoided. The problem could arise in particular in the case of life-assurance companies, which have a strong presence on the occupational pension market (through group contracts) in some Member States. The establishment of a genuine prudential framework should in itself largely eliminate the risks of distortion of competition. The draft also provides that institutions that are similar in some respects to life-assurance companies (in that they give an interest-rate guarantee and/or cover biometric risks) will also be the subject of equivalent provisions for own funds (see in particular Article 17). In addition, the Directive gives the possibility to Member States to apply the prudential requirements of this Directive to the occupational pension business of life-assurance companies.

Article 5 – Small pension schemes and statutory schemes

A *de minimis provision* is proposed, as an option for Member States, for IORPs managing small pension schemes. These institutions are likely to be not interested in any form of cross-border activity. Such a provision could facilitate supervision in Member States where tens of thousands of occupational pension schemes are in place.

In some Member States, occupational retirement provision can be operated by institutions which are covered by a public authority with revenue raising powers. Such a cover is deemed to be sufficient for the protection of members and beneficiaries.

Article 6 – Definitions

- This Directive is intended to apply to employment-related institutions for pension provision that operate on a funded basis. These are the last major financial institutions which are not covered by an EU regulatory framework allowing them to benefit from the Single Market. The notion of ‘institution for occupational retirement provision’ was chosen because it seems generic enough to cater for the diversity of institutions operating in the Union. The notion of 'pension funds', for instance, is not common to all Member States. Some of these institutions may also offer services not only to undertakings but also directly to employees or self-employed persons. The Directive is designed to cover such situations.

• The 'sponsoring undertaking' is usually characterised by the fact that it pays contributions into the institution for retirement provision. It can happen, however, that sponsoring undertakings are granted 'contribution holidays' because the returns on investment are sufficient to cover the costs. It can also happen that a specific benefit is fully financed by contributions paid by employees. It is understood that these exceptional circumstances do not impact on the validity of the definition.

The definition of 'retirement benefits' needs to be sufficiently wide in order to cover the various operations carried out by the institutions concerned.

Article 7 – Activities of the institutions

The protection of beneficiaries requires that the IORPs limit their activities to those that will be supervised under the future Directive.

Article 8 – Separation between the sponsoring undertaking and the institution

In the absence of a guarantee or insolvency insurance, legal separation between the undertaking and the IORP is a key element affording beneficiaries protection. This separation in no way prevents the board of an institution of consisting of both the employer and the employees of the company.

Article 9 – Conditions of operation

The essential point for adequate protection of members and beneficiaries of a pension scheme is prudential supervision by a competent authority that can monitor the conditions of operations of IORPs on the basis of the following criteria: competence and good repute of managers, directors and all persons controlling the institution, existence of rules regarding the functioning of the scheme, proper calculation of technical provisions by an actuary or other specialist in this field on the basis of recognised actuarial methods, contractual commitment on the part of the sponsoring undertaking and sufficient information to be given to members on the conditions of operations of the pension scheme (contractual rights and obligations, risks embedded in the pension contract and distribution of the risks among the contracting parties). In case of cross border activity an IORP needs a prior authorisation granted by the competent authority of the home Member State.

Article 10 – Annual accounts and annual report

The annual accounts and the annual report, approved in good and due form by the competent persons, shall constitute the basis for ongoing financial supervision of the IORP by competent authorities.

Article 11 – Information to be given to the members and beneficiaries of the scheme

Proper information is a vital element for the protection of those who have already retired (beneficiaries) and those who will retire in future (members). However, the contents of information shall differ with respect to the recipient (member or beneficiary) and to the contractual conditions of the pension scheme concerned. On request the annual accounts and the annual report shall be made available to members and beneficiaries of the scheme

Article 12 – Disclosure of investment policy

It is proposed that IORPs disclose every three years, and in any case following a significant change in the investment policy, information on the principles underlying their investment policy with respect to the nature and duration of pension liabilities. This information shall also include a description of the risk measurement methods and risk management processes implemented. The statement of investment policy principles is addressed to the supervisory authorities who verify the coherence of actual investments with the principles spelt out. Such a document is one way of obliging managers to take a detached view of the asset-liability management processes and to put their overall investment strategy into perspective. On request this statement of investment policy principles shall be also be sent to members and beneficiaries of the scheme.

Article 13 – Information to be provided to the competent authority

This Article ensures that the supervisory authorities are sufficiently equipped with information rights to perform their responsibilities properly and safeguard the interests of members and beneficiaries of the scheme.

Article 14 – Powers of intervention of the competent authority

This Article ensures that the supervisory authorities are sufficiently equipped with powers of intervention to perform their responsibilities properly and safeguard the interests of members and beneficiaries of the scheme. The competent authorities may carry out on-site-inspections at the IORPs premises and, where appropriate, on outsourced functions.

Article 15 – Technical provisions

In order to safeguard the interests of members and beneficiaries, institutions must establish technical provisions. In cases where the institutions operate schemes in which biometric risks are covered and/or where the institution bears the investment risk, the technical provisions must be calculated on a sufficiently prudent basis.

The calculation of technical provisions shall take place every year and shall be executed and certified by qualified actuaries according to recognised actuarial methods. This calculation of technical provisions may take place once every three years if the IORP provides the competent authority with a certification of adjustments for the intervening years.

The interest rate shall be chosen prudently according to national rules and the amount of technical provisions shall both reflect an actuarial value of accrued pension rights of members and must be sufficient for pensions and benefits already in payment to beneficiaries to continued to be paid.

Article 16 – Funding of technical provisions

In principle, the technical provisions must be fully covered by appropriate assets at all times. However, given the very long-term nature of investments by IORPs and the lower exposure to liquidity risks (stemming from the absence of any redemption possibility, unlike in the insurance field) Member States may permit IORPs, for a limited period, to depart from the full funding requirement. Any departure must be accompanied by a plan to re-establish full cover of the technical provisions.

In the event of cross-border activity the technical provisions must be fully funded at all times to protect the interests of members and beneficiaries of the scheme and in order to allow mutual recognition of the different supervisory regimes established in Member States.

Article 17 – Regulatory own funds

In many cases, it is the sponsoring undertaking and not the IORP itself that either covers any biometric risk or guarantees certain benefits or investment performance. However, in some cases it is the IORP itself which provides such cover or guarantees and the sponsors obligations are generally exhausted by paying the necessary contributions. In these circumstances, the products offered are similar to those of life-insurance companies. The draft requires IORPs offering such products to hold the same additional own funds as life-assurance companies.

Article 18 – Investment rules

A qualitative approach to investment rules is proposed. This is because it is deemed preferable for the allocation of assets to be decided in the light of the liabilities entered into by each fund and not in the light of a single set of quantitative rules. As a general rule, asset allocation must be prudent. This requires, above all, a proper diversification in terms of issuers, types of securities, country/geographical zone, currency and industrial sector. In case of significant investments in the sponsoring undertaking, bankruptcy of that undertaking could have the double effect of depriving employees from their job and jeopardising their pension rights. Self-investment therefore needs to be strictly limited.

Supervisory methods differ a lot from one Member State to another. Therefore, Member States should be given some discretion on the precise investment rules that they wish to require from institutions established in their territories. Such an approach was already adopted in the insurance Directives (see, for instance, Article 22(2) of Directive 92/96/EEC). IORPs are very long-term investors ideally placed to take advantage of the high returns and low volatility traditionally offered over the long term by shares. They need to link pension promises to the long term growth of the real economy. They also need to benefit from international diversification and undertake investments in currencies other than those in which their liabilities are denominated. Such investments should therefore not be restricted excessively.

As very long-term investors, IORPs can help improve the size and liquidity of EU risk capital markets. It is for the IORP itself to decide whether it wishes or not to invest in risk capital. It is therefore essential that the regulatory framework does not excessively restrict this form of investment.

Article 19 – Management and custody

Under this Article, IORPs are free to delegate the management and custodial services to institutions duly approved in another Member State. This article secures the application of the principle of free provision of services for credit institutions and asset managers.

Article 20 – Cross-border activities

The coordination of prudential supervision is one of the necessary conditions for allowing an IORP to manage schemes on a cross-border basis. A greater degree of tax coordination is also essential. This matter is not dealt with in this proposal. Article 20 simply lays down the principle of freedom of cross-border activities and proposes a mechanism for cooperation and notification between supervisory authorities. The Article also establishes that an IORP wishing to manage a scheme in another Member State will have to apply the relevant social and labour law requirements of the Member State where the sponsoring company is established. These requirements essentially relate to what retirement benefits need to be provided.

Notes

[1] SEC(98) 552 final.
[2] COM(93) 237 final
[3] Directives 93/22/EEC, 2000/12/EC and 92/96/EEC.
[4] COM(1998) 451
[5] COM(97) 283.
[6] COM(1999) 134
[7] Resolution A5-0053/2000
[8] COM(1999) 232.

2000/0260 (COD)

Proposal for a

Directive of the European Parliament and of the Council

on the activities of institutions for occupational retirement provision

(Text EEA relevance)

Commission of the European Communities

THE EUROPEAN PARLIAMENT AND THE COUNCIL OF THE EUROPEAN UNION,

Having regard to the Treaty establishing the European Community, and in particular Articles 47(2), 55 and 95(1) thereof,

Having regard to the proposal from the Commission,[1]

Having regard to the opinion of the Economic and Social Committee,[2]

Acting in accordance with the procedure laid down in Article 251 of the Treaty,[3]

Whereas:

(1) A genuine internal market for financial services is crucial for economic growth and job creation in the Community.

(2) Major achievements have already been made in the establishment of this internal market, allowing financial institutions to operate in other Member States and ensuring a high level of protection for the consumers of financial services.

(3) The Communication from the Commission implementing the framework for financial markets: action plan[4] identifies a series of actions that are needed in order to complete the internal market for Financial Services and the European Council at its meeting in Lisbon on 23 and 24 March 2000, called for the implementation of this Action Plan by 2005.

(4) The Action Plan for Financial Services stresses as an urgent priority the need to draw up a Directive on the prudential supervision of institutions for occupational retirement provision, as these institutions are major financial institutions not subject to a coherent Community legislative framework allowing them to fully benefit from the advantages of the internal market.

(5) Institutions that are completely separated from any sponsoring undertaking and that operate on a funded basis for the sole purpose of providing retirement benefits should have freedom to provide services and freedom of investment subject only to coordinated prudential requirements, regardless of whether these institutions are considered as legal entities.

(6) Member States should retain full responsibility for the organisation of their social protection systems.

(7) Institutions managing social security schemes, which are already coordinated at Community level, should be excluded from the scope of this Directive. Account should nevertheless be taken of the specificity of institutions which, in a single Member State, manage both social security schemes and occupational schemes.

(8) Financial institutions that already benefit from a Community legislative framework should in general be excluded from the scope of this Directive. However, as these institutions may also in some cases offer occupational pension services, it is important to ensure that this Directive does not lead to distortions of competition. Such distortions may be avoided by applying the prudential requirements of this Directive to the occupational pension business of life-assurance companies.

(9) Giving Member States the possibility to exclude from the scope of national implementing legislation institutions managing schemes with less than 100 members or beneficiaries can facilitate supervision in some Member States without undermining the proper functioning of the internal market in this field.

(10) Institutions such as Unterstützungskassen in Germany, where the members have no legal rights

to benefits of a certain amount and where their interests are protected by a compulsory statutory insolvency insurance, should be excluded from the scope of the Directive.

(11) In order to protect members and beneficiaries, institutions for occupational retirement provision should limit their activities to the activities, and operations arising therefrom, referred to in this Directive.

(12) In case of bankruptcy of an undertaking which pays contributions into an institution, a sponsoring undertaking, the member faces the risk of losing both his job and his acquired pension rights. This makes it necessary to ensure that there is a clear separation between that undertaking and the institution.

(13) Institutions for occupational retirement provision operate and are supervised with significant differences in Member States. In some Member States, supervision can be exercised not only on the institution itself but also on the companies that are authorised to manage these institutions. Member States should be able to take such specificity into account as long as all the requirements laid down in this Directive are effectively met.

(14) Institutions for occupational retirement provision are financial service providers and therefore should meet certain minimum prudential standards with respect to their activities and conditions of operation.

(15) The huge number of institutions in certain Member States means a pragmatic solution is necessary as regards prior authorisation of institutions. However, if an institution wants to manage a scheme in another Member State, a prior authorisation granted by the competent authority of the home Member State should be required.

(16) The annual accounts and annual report, reflecting a true and fair view of the institution's assets, liabilities and financial position duly approved by an authorised person responsible for auditing the annual accounts, are an essential source of information for members and beneficiaries of the scheme and the competent authorities. In particular, they enable the competent authorities to monitor the financial soundness of an institution and assess whether the institution is able to meet all its contractual obligations.

(17) Proper information of members and beneficiaries of the pension scheme is crucial. This is of particular relevance for information requests concerning the financial soundness of the institution, the contractual rules, the benefits and the actual financing of accrued pension entitlements, the investment policy and the management of risks and costs.

(18) The investment policy of an institution is a decisive factor for both security and affordability of occupational pensions. The institutions should therefore draw up, at least every three years, a statement of investment principles. It should be sent to the competent authority and made available on request also to members and beneficiaries of the scheme.

(19) To fulfil their statutory function, competent authorities should be provided with adequate rights to information and powers of intervention with respect to the institution and the persons who effectively run the institution. In case the institution for occupational retirement provision has transferred functions of material importance such as investment management, informatics or accounting to other companies (outsourcing), it should be possible for the rights to information and powers of intervention to be enlarged to these outsourced functions to check if activities are carried out in accordance with the supervisory rules.

(20) A prudent calculation of technical provisions is an essential condition to ensure that obligations to pay retirement benefits can be met. Technical provisions should be calculated on the basis of recognised actuarial methods and certified by qualified persons. The interest rate should be chosen prudently according to national rules. The amount of technical provisions should both reflect an actuarial value of accrued pension rights of members and be sufficient for benefits already in payment to beneficiaries to continued to be paid.

(21) Risks covered by institutions vary significantly from one Member State to another. Member States should therefore have the possibility to make the calculation of technical provisions subject to additional and more detailed rules than those laid down in this Directive.

(22) Sufficient and appropriate assets to cover the technical provisions protect the interests of members and beneficiaries of the pension scheme if the sponsoring undertaking becomes insolvent. In particular in cases of cross-border activity, the mutual recognition of supervisory principles applied in Member States requires that the technical provisions be fully funded at all times.

(23) If the institution does not work on a cross-border basis, Member States should be able to permit underfunding provided that a proper plan is established to restore full funding and without prejudice to the requirements of Council Directive 80/987/EEC of 20 October 1980 on the approximation of the laws of the Member States relating to the protection of employees in the event of the insolvency of their employer.[5]

(24) In many cases, it is the sponsoring undertaking and not the institution itself that either covers any

biometric risk or guarantees certain benefits or investment performance. However, in some cases, it is the institution itself which provides such cover or guarantees and the sponsor's obligations are generally exhausted by paying the necessary contributions. In these circumstances, the products offered are similar to those of life-insurance companies and the institutions concerned should hold the same additional own funds as life-assurance companies.

(25) Institutions are very long-term investors. Redemption of the assets held by these institutions cannot, in general, be made for another purpose than providing retirement benefits. Furthermore, in order to adequately protect the rights of members and beneficiaries, institutions should be able to opt for an asset allocation that suits the precise nature and duration of their liabilities. These aspects call for a qualitative approach towards investment rules, obliging institutions to act prudently but also allowing them sufficient flexibility to decide on the most secure and efficient investment policy.

(26) Supervisory methods and practises vary among Member States. Therefore, Member States should be given some discretion on the precise investment rules that they wish to require from the institutions established in their territories. However, these rules must not restrict the free movement of capital, unless justified on prudential grounds.

(27) As very long-term investors with low-liquidity risks, institutions for occupational retirement provision are in a position to invest in non-liquid assets such as shares as well as in risk capital markets. They can also benefit from the advantages of international diversification. Investments in shares, risk capital markets and currencies other than those of the liabilities should therefore not be unduly restricted.

(28) Restrictions regarding the free choice of approved asset managers and custodians limit competition in the internal market and should therefore be eliminated.

(29) Institutions should have the possibility to provide their services in other Member States. This would potentially lead to significant economies of scale for these institutions, improve the competitiveness of the Community industry and facilitate labour mobility. This requires mutual recognition of prudential standards.

(30) The right for an institution in one Member State to manage an occupational pension scheme concluded in another Member State should be exercised while fully respecting the provisions of the local social and labour law in force in the host Member State.

(31) In accordance with the principles of subsidiarity and proportionality as set out in Article 5 of the Treaty, the objectives of the proposed action, namely to create a Community legal framework covering institutions for occupational retirement provisions, cannot be sufficiently achieved by the Member States and can therefore, by reason of the scale and effects of the action, be better achieved by the Community. This Directive confines itself to the minimum required in order to achieve those objectives and does not go beyond what is necessary for that purpose,

HAVE ADOPTED THIS DIRECTIVE:

Article 1

Subject-matter

This Directive lays down rules for taking up and pursuit of activities carried out by institutions for occupational retirement provision.

Article 2

Scope

This Directive shall apply to institutions for occupational retirement provision.

It shall not apply to:

(a) institutions managing social security schemes that are covered by Council Regulation (EEC) No 1408/71[6], or are listed in Annex II thereto, and Council Regulation (EEC) No 574/72[7];

(b) institutions that are covered by Council Directive 79/267/EEC[8], Council Directive 85/611/EEC[9], Council Directive 93/22/EEC[10] and Directive 2000/12/EC of the European Parliament and of the Council[11];

(c) institutions that operate on a pay-as-you-go basis;

(d) German 'Unterstützungskassen' and other institutions operating in a similar way;

(e) companies using book-reserve schemes with a view to paying-out pension benefits to their employees.

Article 3

Application to institutions operating social security schemes

Institutions for occupational retirement provision that also operate compulsory employment related pension schemes which are considered to be social security schemes covered by Regulations (EEC) No 1408/71 and (EEC) No 574/72 shall be covered by this Directive in respect of their non-compulsory occupational retirement provision activities.

Article 4

Optional application to institutions covered by Directive 79/267/EEC

Member States may choose to apply Articles 11 to 16, 18 to 19 of this Directive to the occupational retirement provision business of activities of institutions that are covered by Directive 79/267/EEC, provided that the relevant assets and liabilities are managed in a separate legal entity. In this case, such separate legal entity shall not be made subject to Articles 17 and 21 of Directive 79/267/EEC and to Articles 19 to 24 and 31 of Council Directive 92/96/EEC[12].

Article 5

Small pension schemes and statutory schemes

1. Member States may choose not to apply this Directive, in whole or in part, to institutions running pension schemes of which less than 100 persons are members and beneficiaries. Article 20 may only be applied if a Member State chooses to apply all the provisions of this Directive to such institutions.

2. Member States may choose not to apply Articles 9 to 17 to institutions where occupational retirement provision is made under statute and which is guaranteed by a public authority.

Article 6

Definitions

For the purposes of this Directive:

(a) 'institution for occupational retirement provision', or 'institution', means an institution operating on a funded basis, established separately from any sponsoring undertaking or trade for the sole purpose of providing retirement benefits in the context of an occupational activity on the basis of an agreement or a contract agreed individually or collectively between the employer(s) and the employee(s) or their respective representatives or between the institution and the individual, both self-employed and employed;

(b) 'pension scheme' means a contract, an agreement, a trust deed or rules stipulating which retirement benefits are granted and under which conditions;

(c) 'sponsoring undertaking' means any undertaking or other body which pays contributions into an institution;

(d) 'retirement benefits' means benefits in the form of payments, whether for life time, a temporary period or as a lump sum, paid on death, disability, cessation of employment or when a defined age is reached, or support payments or services in case of sickness, indigence or death when they are supplementary to those benefits;

(e) 'members' means the persons entitled, or who will be entitled, to receive retirement benefits;

(f) 'beneficiaries' means the persons receiving retirement benefits;

(g) 'competent authorities' means the national authorities designated to carry out the duties provided for in this Directive;

(h) 'biometrical risks' means risks linked to human life. This includes death, disability and longevity risks;

(i) 'risk capital markets' means markets providing equity financing to a company during its early growth stages;

(j) 'home Member State' means the Member State in which the institution is located;

(k) 'host Member State' means the Member State where the sponsoring undertaking or the individual member (s) are located;

(l) 'location':

- where an institution is concerned, the Member State where it has its registered office or its main administration;
- where a sponsoring undertaking is concerned, the Member State in which it has its registered office or its main administration if that sponsoring undertaking is a legal person, a branch or an agency or the Member State in which its head office is situated if that sponsoring undertaking is a natural person;
- where an individual is concerned, the Member State in which he or she has his or her residence.

Article 7

Activities of the institution

Member States shall require institutions located within their territories to limit their activities to retirement benefits related operations and activities directly arising therefrom, including activities arising from their investment policy.

Article 8

Legal separation between the sponsoring undertaking and the institution for occupational retirement provision

Member States shall ensure that there is a legal separation between the sponsoring undertaking and the institution for occupational retirement provision in order that the assets of the institution are safeguarded in the interest of the members and beneficiaries, in the event of bankruptcy of the sponsoring undertaking.

Article 9

Conditions of operation

1. Member States shall ensure that:

(a) the institution is registered;

(b) the institution is effectively run by persons of good repute who must themselves have appropriate professional qualifications and experience or employ advisers with appropriate professional qualifications and experience;

(c) proper constituted rules regarding the functioning of the pension scheme have been implemented and members have been adequately informed of these rules;

(d) all technical provisions are computed and certified by an actuary or other specialist in this field on the basis of recognised actuarial methods;

(e) if the sponsoring undertaking guarantees the payment of the retirement benefits it must be committed to regular financing;

(f) the members are sufficiently informed of the conditions of the pension scheme, in particular concerning:

(i) the contractual rights and obligations of the parties involved in the pension scheme;

(ii) the financial, technical and other risks embedded in the pension contract;

(iii) the distribution of the risks embedded in the pension contract to the contractual parties.

2. Member States may make the conditions of operation of an institution subject to other requirements, with a view to ensuring that the interests of members and beneficiaries are adequately protected.

3. In case of cross-border activity as referred to in Article 20, the conditions of operation of the institution shall be subject to a prior authorisation by the competent authority of the home Member State.

Article 10

Annual accounts and annual report

Member States shall require that institutions located in their territories draw up annual accounts and an annual report. The annual accounts and the annual report shall give a true and fair view of the institution's assets, liabilities and financial position. They shall be consistent and duly approved by an authorised person responsible for auditing the annual accounts.

Article 11

Information to be given to the members and beneficiaries of the scheme

1. Depending on the nature of the pension scheme established, Member States shall ensure that the information set out in paragraphs 2, 3 and 4 is provided.

2. Members and beneficiaries shall receive:

(a) on request, the annual accounts and the annual report;

(b) within a reasonable time, any relevant information regarding changes to the pension scheme rules.

3. Each member shall receive on request, detailed and substantial information on:

(a) if applicable, the target level of the benefits;

(b) the actual financing of accrued pension entitlements;

(c) the level of benefits in case of termination of employment;

(d) where the member bears the investment risk, the range of investment possibilities and the actual investment portfolio as well as information on risk exposure and costs related to the investments.

Information on issues set out in the first subparagraph shall be provided together with the annual accounts and the annual report as mentioned in paragraph 2(a).

4. Each beneficiary shall be provided with the appropriate information on the retirement benefits that are due and the corresponding payment options.

Article 12

Disclosure of investment policy principles

1. Member States shall ensure that every three years, as well as without delay after any significant change in the investment policy, all institutions located in their territories disclose their investment policies to the competent authority of the home Member State. This shall be done by sending a statement of investment policy principles containing the risk measurement methods and risk management processes implemented and the strategic asset allocation with respect to the nature and duration of pension liabilities.

2. The statement of investment policy principles shall also be made available to members and beneficiaries of the scheme on request.

Article 13

Information to be provided to the competent authority

Every Member State shall ensure that the competent authority has the necessary powers and means:

(a) to require the institution, the members of their boards of directors and other managers or directors or persons controlling the institution to supply information about all business matters or forward all business documents;

(b) to supervise contracts regulating relationships between the institution and other companies, transferring functions to other companies (outsourcing), influencing the financial situation of the institution or being in a material way relevant for effective supervision;

(c) to obtain regularly, in addition to the annual accounts and the annual report, all the documents necessary for the purposes of supervision in particular:

(i) internal interim reports:

(ii) actuarial valuations;

(iii) asset-liability studies;

(iv) evidence of coherence with the investment policy principles;

(v) evidence that contributions have been paid in as planned;

(vi) report of the statutory auditor;

(d) to carry out on-site inspections at the institution's premises and, where appropriate, on outsourced functions to check if activities are carried out in accordance with the supervisory rules.

Article 14

Powers of intervention of the competent authority

1. The competent authority shall require every institution to have sound administrative and accounting procedures and adequate internal control mechanisms.

2. The competent authority may take any measures, with regard to the institution or the persons running the institution, that are appropriate and necessary to prevent or remedy any irregularities prejudicial to the interests of the members and beneficiaries.

It may also restrict or prohibit the free disposal of the institution's assets when:

(a) the institution has failed to establish sufficient technical provisions in respect of the entire business or insufficient assets to cover the technical provisions;

(b) the institution has failed to hold the regulatory own funds.

3. In order to safeguard the interests of scheme members and beneficiaries, the competent authority may transfer the powers which the persons running the institution hold in accordance with the law or its statutes wholly or partly to a special representative who is fit to execute these powers.

4. The competent authority may prohibit or restrict the activities of the institution in particular if:

(a) the institution fails to adequately protect the interests of scheme members and beneficiaries;

(b) the institution no longer fulfils the conditions of operations;

(c) the institution fails seriously in its obligations under the rules to which it is subject;

(d) in case of cross-border activity the institution does not respect the provisions of labour and social law of the host Member State relevant in the field of occupational pensions. Any decision to prohibit activities of the institution shall be supported by precise reasons and notified to the institution in question.

5. In case of cross-border activity as referred to in Article 20, the institution shall be subject to ongoing supervision by the competent authority of the host Member State as to the compliance of its activities with the labour and social law requirements of the host Member State referred to in Article 20(5).

6. Member States shall ensure that decisions taken in respect of an institution under laws, regulations and administrative provisions adopted in accordance with this Directive are subject to the right to apply to the courts.

Article 15

Technical provisions

1. Member States shall ensure that institutions operating occupational pension schemes establish at all times the adequate amount of liabilities to reflect the financial commitments that arise out of their portfolio of existing pension contracts.

2. Member States shall ensure that institutions operating occupational pension schemes that provide cover against biometric risks and/or where the benefits include a guarantee of either investment performance or level of benefits establish sufficient technical provisions in respect of the total range of these schemes.

3. The calculation of technical provisions shall take place every year. However, Member States may allow a calculation once every three years if the institution provides the competent authority with a certification of adjustments for the intervening years. The certification shall reflect the adjusted development of the technical provisions and changes in risks covered.

4. The calculation of the technical provisions shall be executed and certified by an actuary or other specialist in this field on the basis of recognised actuarial methods according to the following principles:

(a) the minimum amount of the technical provisions shall be calculated by a sufficiently prudent actuarial valuation. It must be sufficient both for pensions and benefits already in payment to beneficiaries to continue to be paid, and to provide members with an actuarial value of their accrued pension rights;

(b) the rate of interest used shall be chosen prudently and determined in accordance with the rules of the competent authority of the home Member State;

(c) the method and basis of calculation of technical provisions shall in general remain constant from one financial year to the other. However, discontinuities may be justified due to a change of legal or economic circumstances underlying the assumptions.

5. Member States may make the calculation of technical provisions subject to additional and more detailed requirements, with a view to ensuring that the interests of members and beneficiaries are adequately protected.

Article 16

Funding of technical provisions

1. Member States shall require every institution to have sufficient and appropriate assets to cover the technical provisions in respect of the total range of schemes operated at all times.

2. Member States may permit institutions for a limited period, to derogate from the provisions of paragraph 1. In order to ensure that the requirements of paragraph 1 are met again, derogation shall be subject to the following conditions:

(a) the institution shall set up a concrete and realisable plan to re-establish the required amount of assets to fully cover the technical provisions in due time. The plan is subject to approval by the competent authority;

(b) in drawing up the plan, account shall be taken of the specific situation of the institution, in particular the asset/liability structure, risk profile, liquidity plan, the age profile of the persons entitled to receive retirement benefits, start-up schemes and schemes changing from non- or partial funding to full funding;

(c) the institution shall establish and disclose to the competent authority a procedure in order to transfer the assets to another financial institution or a similar body in the event of the termination of the pension scheme during the derogation period.

3. In the event of cross-border activity as referred to in Article 20, the technical provisions must be fully funded at all times.

Article 17

Regulatory own funds

1. Member States shall ensure that institutions operating pension schemes where the institution itself underwrites the liability to cover a biometric risk and/or where the institution itself guarantees an investment performance or a given level of benefits hold, on a permanent basis, additional assets above the technical provisions in respect of the total range of schemes operated. These assets shall be free of all foreseeable liabilities and serve as a safety capital to absorb discrepancies between the anticipated and the actual expenses and profits.

2. For the purposes of calculating the amount of the additional assets, the rules laid down in Directive 79/267/EEC shall apply.

Article 18

Investment rules

1. Member States shall require institutions established within their jurisdiction to invest in a prudent manner.

2. Assets held in relation to schemes where the members bear the investment risks shall be invested in accordance with the following rules:

(a) the assets shall be invested in a manner to ensure the security, quality, liquidity and profitability of the portfolio as a whole;

(b) the assets shall be properly diversified in such a way as to avoid accumulations of risk in the portfolio as a whole;

(c) investment in the sponsoring undertaking shall be no more than 5 per cent of the portfolio as a whole. When the institution is sponsored by a group of undertakings, investment in these sponsoring undertakings shall be made prudently, taking into account the need for proper diversification.

3. Member States shall require institutions established within their jurisdiction to invest assets

held to cover the technical provisions in accordance with the following rules:

(a) the assets shall be invested in a manner appropriate to the nature and duration of the expected future retirement benefits and to ensure the security, quality, liquidity and profitability of the portfolio as a whole;

(b) the assets shall be properly diversified in such a way as to avoid accumulations of risk in the portfolio as a whole;

(c) investment in the sponsoring undertaking shall be no more than 5 per cent of the technical provisions. When the institution is sponsored by a group of undertakings, investment in these sponsoring undertakings shall be made prudently, taking into account the need for proper diversification.

4. Member States shall not require institutions to invest in particular categories of assets.

5. Member States shall not subject the investment decisions of an institution or its investment manager to any kind of prior approval or systematic notification requirements.

6. In accordance with the provisions of paragraphs 1 to 5, Member States may, for the institutions established in their jurisdiction, lay down more detailed rules to reflect the total range of schemes operated by these institutions.

However, these institutions shall be given the possibilities to:

(a) invest up to 70 per cent of the assets covering the technical provisions or of the whole portfolio for schemes in which the members bear the investment risks in shares, negotiable securities treated as shares and corporate bonds and decide on the relative weight of these securities in their investment portfolio;

(b) hold assets denominated in non-matching currencies to cover an amount of at least 30 per cent of their technical provisions;

(c) invest in risk capital markets.

7. The second subparagraph of paragraph 6 does not preclude the right for Member States to require the application of more stringent investment rules on an individual basis provided they are prudentially justified, in particular in light of the liabilities entered into by the institution.

Article 19

Management and custody

1. Member States shall not restrict institutions from appointing, for the management of the investment portfolio, investment managers established in another Member State and duly authorised for this activity, in accordance with Directives 92/96/EEC, 93/22/EEC and 2000/12/EC.

2. Member States shall not restrict institutions from appointing, for the custody of their assets, custodians established in another Member State and duly authorised in accordance with Directive 93/22/EEC or Directive 2000/12/EC, or accepted as a depository for the purposes of Directive 85/611/EEC.

Article 20

Cross-border activities

1. Member States shall allow the undertakings and individuals located within their territories to sponsor institutions for occupational retirement provision authorised in other Member States. They shall also allow institutions for occupational retirement provision authorised in their territory to accept sponsorship by sponsors located within the territories of other Member States.

2. If an undertaking or individuals wish to sponsor an institution authorised in another Member State, this institution shall notify the competent authorities of the Member State where it is authorised.

3. The Member States shall require institutions proposing to be sponsored by an undertaking or individuals located in the territory of another Member State to provide the following information when effecting the notification:

(a) the Member State within the territory of which the sponsoring undertaking or the individuals are located;

(b) the name of the sponsoring undertaking;

(c) the conditions of the scheme that the institution proposes to manage in the host Member State.

4. Unless the competent authorities of the home Member State have reason to doubt that the administrative structure, the financial situation of the institution or the good repute and professional qualifications or experience of the persons running the institution is not compatible with the operations proposed in the host Member State, they shall within three months of receiving all the information referred to in paragraph 3 communicate that information to the competent authorities of the host Member State.

5. Before the institution starts managing a scheme in the host Member State, the competent authorities of the host Member State shall, within two months of receiving the information referred to in paragraph 3, inform the competent authority of the home Member State, if appropriate, of the relevant social

and labour law requirements under which this scheme must be managed in the host Member State. The competent authorities of the home Member State shall communicate this information to the institution.

6. On receiving the communication referred to in paragraph 5, or if no communication is received from them on expiry of the period provided for in the paragraph 5, the institution may start to manage the scheme in the host Member State in accordance with the provisions of the relevant local social and labour law.

7. The competent authorities of the host Member State shall inform the competent authorities of the home Member State of any change regarding the characteristics of the scheme that is managed in the host Member State.

Article 21

Implementation

1. Member States shall bring into force the laws, regulations and administrative provisions necessary to comply with this Directive by 31 December 2003 at the latest. They shall forthwith inform the Commission thereof.

When Member States adopt those provisions, they shall contain a reference to this Directive or be accompanied by such a reference on the occasion of their official publication. Member States shall determine how such reference is to be made.

2. Member States shall communicate to the Commission the text of the main provisions of domestic law which they adopt in the field governed by this Directive.

Article 22

Entry into force

This Directive shall enter into force on the twentieth day following that of its publication in the *Official Journal of the European Communities*.

Article 23

Addressees

This Directive is addressed to the Member States.

Done at Brussels,

For the European Parliament	For the Council
The President	*The President*

Notes

[1] OJ C

[2] OJ C

[3] OJ C

[4] COM(1999) 232 final.

[5] OJ L 283, 28.10.1980, p. 23; Directive as last amended by Directive 87/164/EEC (OJ L 66, 11.3.1987, p. 11).

[6] OJ L 149, 5.7.1971, p. 2.

[7] OJ L 74, 27.3.1972, p. 1.

[8] OJ L 63, 13.3.1979, p. 1.

[9] OJ L 375, 31.12.1985, p. 3.

[10] OJ L 141, 11.6.1993, p. 27.

[11] OJ L 126, 26.5.2000, p. 1.

[12] OJ L 360, 9.12.1992, p. 1.

Progress report to the Ecofin Council on the Impact of ageing populations on public pension systems[1]

Economic Policy Committee

Summary, assessment and future work

Background

In February 2000, ECOFIN asked the Economic Policy Committee (EPC) to prepare a first progress report on the impact of ageing populations on public pension systems by December 2000.

The March 2000 Special European Council in Lisbon gave a '... *mandate [to] the High Level Working Party on Social Protection, taking into consideration the work being done by the Economic Policy Committee, to .... prepare a study on the future evolution of social protection from a long-term point of view, giving particular attention to the sustainability of pensions systems in different time frameworks up to 2020 and beyond, where necessary. A progress report should be available by December 2000.*'

It also requested '... *the Council and the Commission, using the existing procedures, to present a report by Spring 2001 assessing the contribution of public finances to growth and employment, and assessing, on the basis of comparable data and indicators, whether adequate concrete measures are being taken in order to .... ensure the long-term sustainability of public finances, examining the different dimensions involved, including the impact of ageing populations, in the light of the report to be prepared by the High Level Working Party on Social Protection.*'

The present progress report has been prepared by the Working Group on the implications of ageing populations (AWG) set up by the EPC in December 1999 to analyse the impact on public finances that should characterise all European countries in the first half of the current century. All Member States were asked to participate in the Working Group recognising the importance of co-operation and co-ordination for the robustness of the analysis and comparability of the projections.[2]

The secretariat of the OECD also co-operates with the work of the AWG, to ensure that its on-going and parallel Paris-based exercise is consistent with this work. This active co-operation also helps avoid unnecessary duplication of effort by the EU members of the OECD's working group.

Beyond including an overview of the main characteristics of the pension systems in Member States, the report illustrates long-term simulations of public pension expenditure on the basis of demographic and macroeconomic assumptions commonly agreed during the AWG's meetings[3] These common assumptions are a first step in an optimal trade-off, in so far as they allow the modellers to take account of certain national features without detracting from the desired comparability or read-across of the results.

Main characteristics of pension systems in Europe

Apart from some exceptions, the pension systems in European countries are characterised by a strong public component, also known as first pillar pensions.[4] In only three Member States (i.e. Denmark, the Netherlands and the UK), is the private component – also known as the second and third pillar – well developed.

Around half of the public pension systems in the European Union offer a universal pension scheme. This is usually means-tested. All Member States have comprehensive public pension systems and – except in the Netherlands – the regimes are labour-market-based covering workers in the private sector, in the public sector, and at least some of the self-employed. The financing system of the public schemes is usually pay-as-you-go (PAYG).[5] However, in many PAYG systems pension benefits are also financed through transfers from the state budget. In three Member States (Denmark, Sweden and Finland) the financing system is partly pre-funded. Funded schemes ensure that contributions are invested in funds for repayment to individuals after they have retired.

In most cases, the eligibility requirements for obtaining old-age benefits include a minimum age limit and a minimum period of contributions. Apart from some notable exceptions, 65 years will be the most common minimum age requirement for old age pensions for both men and women after 2004. The requirements for the minimum number of contribution years are much more varied across countries and this is not expected to change significantly in the near future. Currently, the average statutory retirement age for old age pensions currently ranges from 60 to 67 but in most countries it is close to 65. However, all Member States - except for the UK - offer early retirement schemes. Such schemes are usually much more generous in terms of their eligibility requirements. The average retirement age for these schemes can be as low as 56 in some Member States. As a result the participation rates in the 55-64 age group are low, even very low in some Member States, compared to international standards for high income countries.

Indexation of pension benefits is sometimes completely prices-based and sometimes completely wage-based. However, in most cases indexation is a mix of the two. In some countries it is also established, ad-hoc, for example during the budget process.

Overview of projections

The AWG took into consideration two main scenarios: a 'current policy' scenario and a 'Lisbon' scenario.

- In the 'current policy' scenario (see chapter 6: Long term simulations of public pensions expenditure), macroeconomic assumptions were commonly agreed during several meetings at the OECD and EU level. These imply convergence of productivity growth in Member States to 1.7-1.8 per cent by the period 2020-2030. They also imply convergence of unemployment rates (although the levels are not assumed to be identical across countries). Participation rates should rise in most countries, especially for women.
- In the 'Lisbon scenario' (see chapter 8: A 'Lisbon' scenario) the macroeconomic assumptions were set in such a way as to model the effects of achieving consistency with the Lisbon European Council conclusions.[6] The European Council conclusions set targets for 2010, but this scenario also assumes that both male and female participation rates and unemployment rates gradually converge to values achieved by the current EU best performers by the middle of the century.[7] In particular, the Lisbon scenario used for projections assumes a further increase of the employment rate of about 10 percentage points (from 70 per cent to 80 per cent) on average in the EU.[8] Moreover, it is assumed that during the first half of the current century European countries will witness convergence of their productivity to the most competitive levels in the world (i.e. the level and growth registered in the US by 2050 where productivity growth is assumed to be around 1 per cent on average in the first half of the current century).

For both scenarios, demographic assumptions for public pension projections were provided by EUROSTAT. In the current policy scenario, the AWG used the mean-variant (or central) demographic projections. They show that starting from around 2020 the EU population is expected to decline, due especially to low fertility rates. By 2050 the population may be more than 3 per cent lower than the current level.

As the so called baby-boomer generation starts to retire, the old age dependency ratio (i.e. the population over 65 as a ratio of working age population) should nearly double from the current 27 per cent to 53 per cent by the middle of the century.

In the Lisbon scenario, the AWG used the high-variant demographic projections.[9] These differ from the mean-variant because they assume higher fertility rates, higher life expectancies at birth and higher net migration levels. In this scenario, the EU population is expected to increase by around 17 per cent from now to 2050. However, it should be noted that for many countries the high-variant demographic projections do not necessarily translate into lower age dependency ratios, as the higher increase in the numbers of young people tends to be compensated by a higher increase in the old.

On the basis of these demographic and macroeconomic scenarios, Member States provided simulations for public pension expenditure as a percentage of GDP. In the current policy scenario this is predicted to rise in all Member States (except in the UK, where it should fall) over the next few decades. In some countries, the rise is substantial. However, the peak is not reached at the same time in all Member States. More precisely:

- In only a handful of Member States do the spending pressures rise slightly, with the peak demand expected to add less than 2 per cent of GDP to pension expenditure, i.e. Italy and Sweden (1.7 per cent, peaking by 2030).
- In the majority of cases the effects of ageing will add roughly 3-5 per cent of GDP to pension expenditure, i.e. Belgium (3.7 per cent, peaking in 2040), Denmark (4.5 per cent, by 2030), Germany (4.3 per cent, by 2050 or after), France (3.9 per cent, by 2030), Ireland (4.4 per cent, by 2050 or after), Austria (3.1 per cent by 2030) and Finland (4.7 per cent, by 2040).
- In a smaller number of cases the upward pressure is even higher, i.e. in Spain the pressure on the pension system could add 8.3 per cent (by 2050 or after), in both the Netherlands and Portugal it could amount to an extra 6.2 per cent of GDP (by 2040 and 2030, respectively).

When the Lisbon scenario is considered, projections show a lower rise of pension expenditure as a percentage of GDP for all countries. The improvement is most pronounced in Portugal (where the change between the year 2000 and the peak year is reduced from 6.2 to 4.1 percentage points of GDP), Belgium (from 3.7 to 1.6 percentage points), and Germany (from 4.3 to 2.3 percentage points). For Sweden and Italy this scenario implies that pension expenditure, as a percentage of GDP, should almost stabilise at 2000 levels. Nevertheless, even in this very favourable scenario the rise of pension expenditures as a percentage of GDP remains high for most countries of the European Union.

The effects on public debt may be significant. An increase in public expenditures on pensions of some 4 to 5 percentage points of GDP, even if spread out over several decades, poses a considerable challenge for the sustainability of public finances and the debt burden. The pressure on public finances could be even greater if health care is taken into account.[10] The impact of health care and these other age-related expenditures will be studied in a next stage of this project. The long-term simulations of the first stage of this project show that the evolution of public debt over the projection period depends not only on the increase in pension expenditures, but upon the level of debt and primary surplus in 2000 (the latter influenced by the cyclical position of the economy in 2000). The results suggest that high debt countries may have problems in meeting the costs of ageing populations if the primary surplus in 2000 - which is assumed to be held constant over the projection period - is relatively low. On the other hand, a rapidly falling debt stock should help lower the interest rate burden and provide some room for increasing pension expenditure. Nevertheless, a lower interest burden may not, in most cases, be sufficient to compensate for all additional age-related expenditure increases.

In some countries, the cost of the pension system is made more sustainable by the presence of a strong funded component. But it should be borne in mind that the such funded components have incurred costs in the past (such as start-up costs) which allow for current benefits. Moves to introduce such systems would have public finance implications. In this respect, it is necessary to study carefully the impact of ageing on such components of the pension system.

More specifically, in Denmark and the Netherlands the second pillar is quite well developed. Such characteristics have a direct positive effect on the public pension system by reducing the burden of ageing populations on first pillar pensions. However, there is also an important indirect implication: taxes on future pension benefits (which are drawn from the private funds) are expected to be quite high and may partially counterbalance the rise in public pension benefits. In Finland, and to some extent in Sweden, the financing of the labour-market-based pension systems is a combination of a fully-funded and a pay-as-you-go system. Pension funds are currently accumulating assets that are also earning interest which – following the assumptions of the simulation – contribute to higher primary surpluses for the general government. This stock of assets, coupled with a high primary surplus, seems to insure the sustainability of the public pensions for these countries in the medium term.[11] In Finland and Sweden the overall tax ratio is, however, high compared with most other EU countries. Scenarios are based on the assumption that these high tax ratios are sustainable.

Member States provided projections using the high-variant and low-variant demographic projections by EUROSTAT. As mentioned earlier, such variants do not necessarily lead to higher or lower rising trends for the old age dependency ratios. As a result, in only a few countries (e.g. in Spain and to a lesser extent Germany) does the high population assumption lead to a visible reduction in the rise of pension expenditures as a percentage of GDP. At the same time, only in Spain and Sweden does the low population variant imply a significant increase in the upward trend of the pension expenditure-GDP ratio.

The AWG also assessed to what extent results were sensitive to assumptions regarding the participation rate, the unemployment rate, productivity growth and the interest rate.

- Regarding the assumptions on the participation rate, sensitivity tests show that a gradual increase (decrease) of participation rates in the order of 5 percentage points above (below) the current policy scenario would imply a lower (higher) rise of the pension expenditure:GDP ratio which ranges in most countries of between 0.3 and 0.8 per cent.[12]

- The sensitivity to assumptions on the unemployment rate is less pronounced. In fact, even a return to levels of the structural unemployment rate around 4-5 per cent would not lead to a pension expenditure:GDP ratio significantly different from the one observed in the current policy scenario. These results confirm the need for European countries to direct labour market policies not only to the reduction of the structural unemployment rate but also to a significant increase in labour force participation. As stressed by the Luxembourg Process and the Lisbon conclusions, substantial margins for improvement are possible if appropriate policies are implemented or reinforced to increase equal opportunities between genders, to eliminate incentives for early retirement for older workers, and to promote school and academic curriculums with better integration between education and work experience.

- The sensitivity analysis on productivity growth assumptions show that Member States can be divided in two broad sub-groups. In some countries (including Spain, Italy, Portugal, Finland, the UK and to a lesser extent Belgium and Sweden), the impact of different productivity growth assumption is relevant. In general, in these countries the link between pension benefits and wages is not contemporaneous so that higher (lower) productivity growth translates only later in higher (lower) pension benefits. In such cases, an acceleration (deceleration) in productivity would lead to a significant decrease (increase) of the rise in pension expenditure:GDP ratio in the short to medium term. In the remaining countries, pension benefits are linked more closely to wage (and, hence, productivity) developments so that the effect of different productivity growth assumptions is practically nil, both in the short and long term. These results point to a greater uncertainty in the projections for the first group of countries given that a wide range of plausible assumptions for productivity growth can be envisaged over the next few decades.

- The impact of the interest rate assumption on public pension expenditure is relevant only in those countries where the public pension system is characterised by a significant fully funded contribution-defined component.[13, 14]

Assessment

The analysis of the Working Group on the Implications of Ageing Populations suggests that demographic developments will soon result in pressures on public pension expenditure. However, the intensity of these effects will vary across Member States. These differences reflect both the different impact and timing of demographic pressures and significant differences between pension regimes in Europe.

Member States should adopt appropriate measures to make sure that such pressures do not undermine the long-term sustainability of their public finances. In some Member States such measures are presently being legislated.

The EPC has studied these issues in the past and has offered a number of recommendations to the Council and Commission in a previous Opinion.[15] To recall, those recommendations suggested:

> (i) The containment of the benefits should represent the main instrument for guaranteeing the solvency of the pay-as-you-go pension system. In order to limit the reduction in the standard of living of the elderly, reforms should primarily aim at delaying retirement.
>
> (ii) The breathing space that pension expenditure projections outline for the next few years should be used to meet the ageing of the baby-boom generation and put it on a sounder fiscal policy footing. Public debt decumulation would also smooth the changes to be implemented in present pension policies.
>
> (iii) The link between social contributions and benefits at the individual level should be strengthened in order to limit the negative effects of contributions and benefits on the labour market and employment.
>
> (iv) The role of funded schemes should be gradually increased. Public policies should support this development by providing a legal and fiscal framework, but without hampering the process of budgetary consolidation.

The analysis that led to these earlier recommendations is still valid. The EPC continues to believe that significant progress could be made if policy choices were to take greater account of these recommendations.

One of the aims of this work is to explore ways to control the possible rising claim of social expenditure on public finances and to compensate for its impact on debt accumulation. This report highlights several.

- One way to achieve this objective is to tighten some of the parameters characterising current eligibility requirements, indexation and benefit calculation for public pensions. In particular, given the low average retirement age and the rising life expectancy of the elderly, reforms in existing pension systems should consider increases in the retirement age especially in early retirement schemes as a priority action point. Increases in the average retirement age have the advantage of smoothing the pension expenditure trend without reducing the living standard of the elderly.[16] Moreover, it should be noted that the 'Lisbon' scenario presented here already makes a number of implicit assumptions about the success of future policies to raise the retirement age in order to boost the labour force.

- It is also clear that measures to improve labour market participation rates, especially amongst women, would have significant positive effects. Higher participation rates would help reduce public debt and go some way to offsetting the need for more severe expenditure cuts or higher tax rates.

- Furthermore, measures designed to improve the participation of older workers (i.e. the over 50s) in the labour market will help to improve Member States' fiscal positions both through higher tax contributions, but also from lower claims on public expenditure from fewer public pensions and unemployment benefit payments.

Another clear option is to restrict the debt accumulation in the longer term, to improve the fiscal position in the next few years before the costs of ageing populations start to bite. Budgetary surpluses and the resulting decrease in debt and the related interest payments would balance the expected increase in pension expenditure.

Finally, all measures conducive to growth in the long run will help to shoulder the burden arising from rising pension expenditures, because a higher standard of living would alleviate tensions from the impact of ageing populations.

Future work

The Working Group intends to investigate the merits of different pension systems and take a more normative approach in its work on ways to stabilise public finances, in the next stage of its work.

Further work will be carried out to assess possible reforms of PAYG and the extent to which the development of funded systems is advisable for European countries and how these can complement existing systems.

The analysis of the Working Group has confirmed the importance of studying (i) the development of privately-run schemes (both collective and individual pension schemes), and (ii) how the increase of the fully funded component of public pension regimes could help in offering better pensions to future generations. These may complement existing PAYG systems while preserving their financial sustainability. But more work is needed to assess both the costs (e.g. a short-run fall in tax revenues where pension fund contributions receive tax breaks, and the higher contribution burden on the changeover generation) and benefits (e.g. the longer-run boost to national savings and knock-on implications for investment) of introducing funded schemes.

In addition, the group is thinking about broadening the scope of its work, to include research on the impact of ageing on healthcare and other age related costs.

Annex 1: Tables: sensitivity analysis

Pension expenditure projections (as a percentage of GDP, Before taxes). High population scenario

	2000	*2005*	*2010*	*2020*	*2030*	*2040*	*2050*	*Change 2000 - Peak Year*
Belgium	9.4	8.8	9.1	10.6	12.3	12.6	12.1	3.2
Denmark	10.3	11.4	12.8	14.2	14.7	13.7	12.8	4.4
Germany	10.3	9.9	9.6	10.8	13.0	13.6	13.3	3.3
Greece[17]	NA	NA	NA	NA	NA	NA	NA	NA
Spain	9.4	9.2	9.3	10.2	12.4	15.1	15.6	6.2
France	12.1	12.2	13.2	15.2	15.8	15.2	NA	3.7
Ireland	4.6	4.6	5.1	6.8	7.5	8.6	8.5	4.0
Italy	14.2	14.1	14.3	14.9	15.6	14.9	12.9	1.4
Luxembourg	NA	NA	NA	NA	NA	NA	NA	NA
Netherlands	7.9	8.2	9.0	11.0	12.7	13.4	13.0	5.5
Austria	14.5	14.3	14.6	15.3	16.7	15 9	14.2	2.2
Portugal	9.4	10.5	11.7	14.3	16.0	15.7	14.3	6.6
Finland	11.3	10.8	11.6	13.8	15.3	15.3	14.8	4.0
Sweden	9.0	8.8	9.2	10.1	10.2	9.9	9.1	1.2
UK	5.1	4.9	4.7	4.5	4.7	4.3	3.7	0.0

Pension expenditure projections (as a percentage of GDP, Before taxes). Low population scenario

	2000	*2005*	*2010*	*2020*	*2030*	*2040*	*2050*	*Change 2000 - Peak Year*
Belgium	9.3	8.7	8.9	10.1	12.1	12.7	12.6	3.4
Denmark[18]	NA	NA	NA	NA	NA	NA	NA	NA
Germany	10.3	9.7	9.5	10.3	12.7	13.6	13.7	3.4
Greece[19]	NA	NA	NA	NA	NA	NA	NA	NA
Spain	9.4	9.1	9.2	10.2	13.2	17.4	19.5	10.1
France	12.1	12.1	13	14.7	15.7	15.8	NA	3.7
Ireland	4.6	4.5	5	6.6	7.6	8.1	9.1	4.5
Italy	14.2	14.1	14.2	14.8	16.1	16.4	14.9	2.2
Luxembourg	NA	NA	NA	NA	NA	NA	NA	NA
Netherlands	7.9	8.2	9	10.9	12.8	13.8	13.4	5.9
Austria	14.5	14.4	14.7	15.8	18.3	18.4	17.4	3.9
Portugal	9.4	10.3	11.3	13.4	14.7	14.3	12.8	5.3
Finland	11.3	10.9	11.8	14.1	15.9	16.3	16.7	5.4
Sweden	9	8.9	9.4	10.7	11.6	12.1	11.7	3.1
UK	5.1	4.9	4.6	4.3	4.6	4.3	3.7	0

Pension expenditure projections (as a percentage of GDP, Before taxes). High participation scenario[20]

	2000	*2005*	*2010*	*2020*	*2030*	*2040*	*2050*	*Change 2000 - Peak Year*
Belgium	NA	NA	NA	NA	NA	NA	NA	NA
Denmark	10.2	11.1	12.2	13.4	14.1	13.5	12.8	3.9
Germany	10.3	9.7	9.4	10.5	13.1	14.2	14.3	4
Greece[21]	NA	NA	NA	NA	NA	NA	NA	NA
Spain	9.4	9.2	9.2	10	12.4	15.5	16.6	7.2
France	12.1	12.2	13.1	14.8	15.5	15.2	NA	3.4
Ireland	4.6	4.6	5	6.5	7.3	7.9	8.6	4
Italy	14.2	14.1	14.2	14.7	15.4	15	13.3	1.2
Luxembourg	NA	NA	NA	NA	NA	NA	NA	NA
Netherlands	7.9	8.2	9	11	12.7	13.4	13	5.5
Austria[22]	NA	NA	NA	NA	NA	NA	NA	NA
Portugal	9.4	10.3	11.4	13.6	15.1	14.9	13.3	5.7
Finland	11.3	10.9	11.6	13.6	15.2	15.4	15.4	4.1
Sweden	NA	NA	NA	NA	NA	NA	NA	NA
UK	5.1	4.9	4.7	4.4	4.7	4.4	3.8	0

Pension expenditure projections (as a percentage of GDP, Before taxes). Low participation scenario[23]

	2000	*2005*	*2010*	*2020*	*2030*	*2040*	*2050*	*Change 2000 - Peak Year*
Belgium	9.4	8.7	9.0	10.6	12.8	13.3	12.9	3.9
Denmark	10.2	11.6	13.1	14.4	15.2	14.4	13.7	5.0
Germany	10.3	9.8	9.5	10.7	13.5	14.7	14.9	4.6
Greece[24]	NA	NA	NA	NA	NA	NA	NA	NA
Spain	9.4	9.2	9.3	10.4	13.4	17.3	18.9	9.5
France	12.1	12.2	13.2	15.2	16.3	16.3	NA	4.2
Ireland	4.6	4.6	5.1	6.8	7.9	8.7	9.6	5.0
Italy	14.2	14.1	14.4	15.3	16.5	16.3	14.4	2.3
Luxembourg	NA	NA	NA	NA	NA	NA	NA	NA
Netherlands	7.9	8.3	9.1	11.3	13.5	14.7	14.3	6.8
Austria[25]	NA	NA	NA	NA	NA	NA	NA	NA
Portugal	10.3	11.4	12.7	15.4	17.3	17.2	15.5	7.0
Finland	11.3	10.9	11.7	14.2	16.0	16.5	16.6	5.3
Sweden	NA	NA	NA	NA	NA	NA	NA	NA
UK	5.1	4.9	4.7	4.5	4.8	4.5	4.0	0.0

Pension expenditure projections (as a percentage of GDP, Before taxes). Low unemployment scenario

	2000	*2005*	*2010*	*2020*	*2030*	*2040*	*2050*	*Change 2000 - Peak Year*
Belgium	9.4	8.7	9.0	10.6	12.0	12.5	12.1	3.1
Denmark	10.2	10.9	12.2	13.4	14.1	13.4	12.8	3.9
Germany	10.3	9.8	9.5	10.6	13.1	14.2	14.2	3.9
Greece[26]	NA	NA	NA	NA	NA	NA	NA	NA
Spain[27]	NA	NA	NA	NA	NA	NA	NA	NA
France	12.1	12.2	13.1	14.8	15.7	15.4	NA	3.6
Ireland	4.6	4.5	5.0	6.6	7.5	8.2	8.9	4.3
Italy	14.2	14.1	14.3	14.9	15.8	15.5	13.7	1.6
Luxembourg	NA	NA	NA	NA	NA	NA	NA	NA
Netherlands	7.9	8.3	9.1	11.3	13.1	14.1	13.6	6.2
Austria	14.5	14.4	14.9	15.8	17.6	17.0	15.1	3.1
Portugal	9.8	10.8	11.9	14.3	15.9	15.7	14.1	6.1
Finland	11.3	10.9	11.6	13.7	15.4	15.6	15.6	4.3
Sweden	9.0	8.8	9.1	10.2	10.6	10.6	9.9	1.6
UK	5.1	4.9	4.6	4.4	4.7	4.4	3.9	0.0

Pension expenditure projections (as a percentage of GDP, Before taxes). High productivity scenario

	2000	*2005*	*2010*	*2020*	*2030*	*2040*	*2050*	*Change 2000 - Peak Year*
Belgium	9.4	8.7	9.0	10.4	12.2	12.5	12.0	3.1
Denmark	10.2	11.3	12.7	14.0	14.7	14.0	13.4	4.5
Germany	10.3	9.8	9.5	10.6	13.1	14.4	14.6	4.3
Greece[28]	NA	NA	NA	NA	NA	NA	NA	NA
Spain	9.4	9.2	9.1	9.6	11.7	14.6	15.4	6.0
France	NA	NA	NA	NA	NA	NA	NA	NA
Ireland	4.6	4.6	5.0	6.7	7.6	8.3	9.1	4.5
Italy	14.2	14.0	13.9	14.1	14.8	14.5	12.9	0.6
Luxembourg	NA	NA	NA	NA	NA	NA	NA	NA
Netherlands	7.9	8.3	9.1	11.1	13.1	14.1	13.7	6.2
Austria	14.6	14.5	14.9	16.0	18.0	1706	15.8	3.4
Portugal	9.8	10.6	11.5	13.4	14.3	13.5	11.7	4.5
Finland	11.3	10.9	11.5	13.4	14.8	14.8	14.7	3.5
Sweden	9.0	8.7	9.0	9.9	10.3	10.1	9.3	1.3
UK	5.1	4.9	4.5	4.1	4.1	3.7	3.1	0.0

Pension expenditure projections (as a percentage of GDP, Before taxes). Low productivity scenario

	2000	2005	2010	2020	2030	2040	2050	Change 2000 - Peak Year
Belgium	NA	NA	NA	NA	NA	NA	NA	NA
Denmark	10.2	11.4	12.7	14.0	14.7	14.0	13.4	4.5
Germany	10.3	9.8	9.5	10.6	13.3	14.5	14.7	4.4
Greece[29]	NA	NA	NA	NA	NA	NA	NA	NA
Spain	9.4	9.2	9.5	10.9	14.2	18.4	20.4	11.0
France	NA	NA	NA	NA	NA	NA	NA	NA
Ireland	4.6	4.6	5.0	6.7	7.6	8.3	9.1	4.5
Italy	14.2	14.2	14.7	15.8	17.1	17.0	15.1	2.9
Luxembourg	NA	NA	NA	NA	NA	NA	NA	NA
Netherlands	7.9	8.3	9.1	11.0	13.1	14.0	13.6	6.1
Austria[30]	NA	NA	NA	NA	NA	NA	NA	NA
Portugal	9.9	11.0	12.4	15.5	18.0	18.6	17.3	8.7
Finland	11.3	10.9	11.9	14.6	16.7	17.3	17.6	6.3
Sweden	9.0	8.8	9.3	10.6	11.3	11.5	10.9	2.5
UK	5.1	4.9	4.8	4.8	5.3	5.3	4.9	0.2

Pension expenditure projections (as a percentage of GDP, Before taxes). High interest rate scenario

	2000	2005	2010	2020	2030	2040	2050	Change 2000 - Peak Year
Belgium	9.3	8.7	9.0	10.4	12.5	13.0	12.6	3.7
Denmark	10.2	11.3	12.6	13.9	14.5	13.8	13.1	4.3
Germany	10.3	9.8	9.5	10.6	13.3	14.4	14.6	4.3
Greece[31]	NA	NA	NA	NA	NA	NA	NA	NA
Spain	9.4	9.2	9.3	10.2	12.9	16.3	17.7	8.3
France	12.1	12.2	13.1	15.0	16.0	15.8	NA	3.9
Ireland	4.6	4.6	5.0	6.7	7.6	8.3	9.1	4.5
Italy	14.2	14.1	14.3	14.9	15.9	15.7	13.9	1.7
Luxembourg	NA	NA	NA	NA	NA	NA	NA	NA
Netherlands	7.9	8.3	9.1	11.1	13.1	14.1	13.6	6.2
Austria	14.5	14.4	14.8	15.7	17.6	17.0	15.1	3.1
Portugal	9.9	10.9	12.2	14.7	16.5	16.4	14.8	6.6
Finland	11.3	10.9	11.6	14.0	15.7	16.0	16.0	4.7
Sweden	9.0	8.8	9.2	10.3	11.0	11.3	10.7	2.3
UK	5.1	4.9	4.7	4.4	4.7	4.4	3.9	0.0

Pension expenditure projections (as a percentage of GDP, Before taxes). Low interest rate scenario

	2000	*2005*	*2010*	*2020*	*2030*	*2040*	*2050*	*Change 2000 - Peak Year*
Belgium	9.3	8.7	9.0	10.4	12.5	13.0	12.6	3.7
Denmark	10.2	11.4	12.7	13.9	14.5	13.8	13.0	4.3
Germany	10.3	9.8	9.5	10.6	13.3	14.4	14.6	4.3
Greece[32]	NA	NA	NA	NA	NA	NA	NA	NA
Spain	9.4	9.2	9.3	10.2	12.9	16.3	17.7	8.3
France	12.1	12.2	13.1	15.0	16.0	15.8	NA	3.9
Ireland	4.6	4.6	5.0	6.7	7.6	8.3	9.1	4.5
Italy	14.2	14.1	14.3	14.9	15.9	15.7	13.9	1.7
Luxembourg	NA	NA	NA	NA	NA	NA	NA	NA
Netherlands	7.9	8.3	9.1	11.1	13.1	14.1	13.6	6.2
Austria	14.5	14.4	14.8	15.7	17.6	17.0	15.1	3.1
Portugal	9.8	10.7	11.9	14.2	15.7	15.5	13.9	5.9
Finland	11.3	10.9	11.6	14.0	15.7	16.0	16.0	4.7
Sweden	9.0	8.8	9.2	10.2	10.5	10.3	9.4	1.5
UK	5.1	4.9	4.7	4.4	4.7	4.4	3.9	0.0

Notes

1 EPC/ECFIN/581/00-EN – Rev.1, BRUSSELS, 6 NOVEMBER, 2000.

2 The members of the group: **Chairman:** Prof. Vittorio GRILLI, Ministero del Tesoro (IT); **Members:** Mr. Henri BOGAERT, Bureau du Plan (B); Mr. Michel ENGLERT, Bureau du Plan (B); Mr. Ulrik NODGAARD, Ministry of Economic Affairs (DK); Mr. Carsten BROGAARD, Ministry of Finance (DK); Ms Britta VELLEUER, Ministry of Finance (D); Mr. Joachim STEINRUCK, Ministry of Labour and Social Affairs (D); Mr. Platon TINIOS, Prime Minister's Office (EL); Ms Daphne NICOLITSAS, Ministry of National Economy (EL); Mr. Juan BURDIEL, Ministerio de Economia Y Hacienda (E); Mr. Juan VARELA, Ministerio de Economia Y Hacienda (E); Mr. Vicente ANTÓN, Ministerio de Economia Y Hacienda (E); Mr. Bernard SALZMANN, Ministère de l'Economie, des Finances et de l'Industrie (F); Ms Claire LOUPIAS, Ministère de l'Economie, des Finances et de l'Industrie (F); Mr. Robert WATT, Department of Finance (IRL); Mr. Serge ALLEGREZZA, Ministère de l'Economie (LUX); Ms Alexandra GUARDA-RAUCHS, Ministère de l'Economie (LUX); Mr. Raymond WAGENER, Inspection Générale de la Securité Sociale (LUX); Mr. Daniele FRANCO, Banca d'Italia (IT); Mr. Francesco MASSICCI, Ragioneria Generale dello Stato (IT); Mr. Rocco APRILE, Ragioneria Generale dello Stato (IT); Mr. H.J.M. TER RELE, CPB - Bureau for Economic Policy Analysis (NL); Mr. Maarten R.P.M. CAMPS, Ministry of Finance (NL); Mr. Peter PART, Ministry of Finance (Ö); Mr. Pedro RODRIGUES, Ministry of Finance (P); Mr. Jorma TUUKKANEN, Ministry of Finance (FI); Mr. Tomas NORDSTRÖM, Ministry of Finance (S); Ms Anna RUDEN, Ministry of Finance (S); Mr. Andrew KILPATRICK, HM Treasury (UK); Mr. Stephen MINERS, HM Treasury (UK); Mr. André DRAMAIS, European Commission (DG-

Economic and Financial Affairs); Mr. Marco BUTI, European Commission (DG-Economic and Financial Affairs); Mr. Declan COSTELLO, European Commission (DG-Economic and Financial Affairs); Mr. Kieran MC MORROW, European Commission (DG-Economic and Financial Affairs); Mr. Jean-Luc ANNAERT, European Commission (DG-Economic and Financial Affairs); Mr. Harri CRUIJSEN, Statistics Netherlands (on behalf of EUROSTAT); Mr. Massimo ROSTAGNO, European Central Bank (ECB); Mr. Howard OXLEY, OECD; Mr. Nicholas VANSTON, OECD; Ms Thai-Thanh DANG, OECD; Mr. Flavio PADRINI, Ministero del Tesoro (IT); Prof. Silvia FEDELI, Ministero del Tesoro (IT); Mr. Alan HOUMANN, EPC Secretariat.

[3] It is important to note that long run simulations of the sort undertaken by the working group involve a considerable degree of uncertainty. On the one hand, projections of the old-age dependency ratio are fairly robust (today's workers and children are already alive and, barring some extreme event, we can calculate the number of pensioners in 50 years time with some accuracy). On the other hand, other demographic variables and economic assumptions have a high degree of uncertainty. Simulations based an a combination of all these factors are thus not forecasts in the usual sense, but are offered as pictures of a number of possible outcomes. Moreover, the limitations of the demographic and economic models themselves necessarily restrict the scope of the analysis. These qualifications must be kept in mind when drawing conclusions from this report.

[4] In this report 'first pillar' indicates public schemes. 'Second pillar' means privately-run pension funds originating in agreements between employers and employees. 'Third pillar' covers individual pension schemes.

[5] In pay-as-you-go (PAYG) schemes the current contributions from workers are used to cover the costs of current payments to pensioners.

[6] The Lisbon European Council Conclusions state that: '...the European Council needs to set a goal for full employment in Europe in an emerging new society which is more adapted to the personal choices of women and men. If the measures set out below are implemented against a sound macro-economic background, an average economic growth rate of around 3 per cent should be a realistic prospect for the coming years.' (Paragraph 6) and also 'The European Council considers that the overall aim of these measures should be, on the basis of the available statistics, to raise the employment rate from an average of 61 per cent today to as close as possible to 70 per cent by 2010 and to increase the number of women in employment from an average of 51 per cent today to more than 60 per cent by 2010. Recognising their different starting points, Member States should consider setting national targets for an increased employment rate. This, by enlarging the labour force, will reinforce the sustainability of social protection systems.' (Paragraph 30).

[7] In some cases, these assumptions might imply a change in the pension eligibility requirements in order to increase labour force participation by the elderly. That is to say, some reform of pension systems is already implicitly assumed in this Lisbon scenario in order to meet the objectives set by the Lisbon European Council.

[8] This assumption implies that countries characterised by lower (higher) starting values for the employment rate should experience an increase of more (less) than 10 percentage points.

[9] Except for Portugal which used the mean-variant scenario.

[10] On the other hand, some other age-related expenditures - such as child allowances and education - could reduce this pressure.

[11] A similar outcome is reached by the creation of an appropriate reserve fund, as currently being tested in France and Spain where contributions are accumulated in order to pay future pension benefits for the baby boom generation. In Ireland a reserve fund has been established on a statutory basis.

[12] More relevant changes are observed in Spain and Portugal.

[13] Of course, changes in the interest rate assumption have an important effect on the corresponding evolution of the debt to GDP ratio. It should also be noted that in some national models a change in real interest rates leads to a different capital labour ratio and, hence, wage levels. On the demand side, GDP is affected by a shift in the demand for investment consequent to an interest rate change. These channels lead to a slightly different evolution of pension expenditure as a percentage of GDP with respect to the current policy scenario.

[14] This component is important only in Sweden where the rise in the pension expenditure:GDP ratio between 2000 and the peak year moves from 1.7 percentage points in the current policy scenario to 2.3, when the interest rate is increased by 1 percentage point (and 1.5 percentage points when it is decreased by 1 percentage point).

[15] Economic Policy Committee, The reform of European pension systems: Opinion Addressed to the Council and Commission (II/220/97-EN final, 6 October 1997).

[16] Depends on the way early retirement schemes are financed. In some states, like the Netherlands, the impact might be neutral.

[17] Greece stated that projections will become available in January 2001.

[18] For this scenario, model's results need further analysis.

[19] Greece stated that projections will become available in January 2001.
[20] In general, higher participation rates have been achieved by raising females' participation rates.
[21] Greece stated that projections will become available in January 2001.
[22] Results could be broadly similar to the Lisbon scenario.
[23] In general, lower participation rates have been achieved by reducing females' participation rates.
[24] Greece stated that projections will become available in January 2001.
[25] Results could be broadly similar to the low population scenario.
[26] Greece stated that projections will become available in January 2001.
[27] Low unemployment already assumed in the current policy scenario.
[28] Greece stated that projections will become available in January 2001.
[29] Greece stated that projections will become available in January 2001.
[30] For this scenario, model's results need further analysis.
[31] Greece stated that projections will become available in January 2001.
[32] Greece stated that projections will become available in January 2001.

The Future Evolution of Social Protection from a Long-Term Point of View: Safe and Sustainable Pensions[1]

Commission of the European Communities[2]

Introduction

Pension systems comprise both public and private schemes and are usually built on three pillars: basic public schemes, occupational schemes and individual pension plans. Each of these pillars has its specific advantages and drawbacks. However, in all Member States, the largest share of older people's income is provided through public pension schemes. The combination of the three pillars making up pension systems offer an unprecedented degree of prosperity and economic independence to older people in Europe. The prospect of population ageing and the retirement of the 'baby boomer' generation represents a major challenge to this historic achievement. Population ageing will be on such a scale that, in the absence of appropriate reforms, it risks undermining the European social model as well as economic growth and stability in the European Union. Member States are therefore invited to set out clear strategies for ensuring the adequacy of their pension systems without destabilising public finances or over-burdening the economy.

While each Member State remains responsible for its pension system, it is clear that they also have much to learn from each other. Furthermore, the sustainability of pension systems will determine to a significant extent the European Union's ability to achieve the promotion of a high level of social protection which is one of the fundamental objectives defined in Article 2 of the Treaty establishing the European Community. This is why the European Council has called for a co-operative exchange on the future sustainability of pension systems. The present communication proposes a framework for taking this work forward.

At its meeting in Lisbon on 23-24 March 2000, the European Council decided to '*mandate the High Level Working Party on Social Protection, taking into consideration the work being done by the Economic Policy Committee, [...] as its first priority, to prepare, on the basis of a Commission communication, a study on the future evolution of social protection from a long-term point of view, giving particular attention to the sustainability of pensions systems in different time frameworks up to 2020 and beyond, where necessary.'*[3] The Lisbon conclusions, referring to the need to modernise social protection, spoke of how '*the challenge can be better addressed as part of a co-operative effort.*'

The European Council discussed pension systems again at its meeting in Santa Maria da Feira on 19-20 June and stressed that '*particular attention should be given to the sustainability of pension schemes through defining two action lines aimed at improved forecasting of future trends and at obtaining in-depth knowledge of recent, actual or expected national pension reform strategies.*'

This communication responds to these requests by addressing the issue of sustainable pensions. Sustainability of pension systems refers to their ability to meet social objectives on an ongoing basis while maintaining other important policy goals, such as sound public finances and intergenerational equity. Sustainability cannot be ensured by one or various elements in isolation. High rates of economic growth and employment increases are crucial and will strongly contribute to sustainability. Together with that, reforms of pension systems as such will contribute to ensuring their sustainability, even more so given the uncertainties linked to the long-term nature of the issue. Such reforms may concern the parameters of public pension schemes as well as the structure of the pension system, i.e. the contributions of three pillars.

The communication is intended to inform the work of the High Level Working Party on Social Protection on the long-term evolution of pensions. It recalls the principal challenges that pension systems will be facing and proposes a framework for analysis of the challenges and policy responses.

Issues relating to pension reform are already high on the agenda in many Member States. A number of Member States have already started reforms which may involve all three pillars of pension systems. Reforms of public pension schemes mainly focus on controlling the growth of expenditure, whereas improvements in occupational and personal pension schemes are often necessary to allow them to play a greater role in income provision for older people. As the systems are different in each Member State a standard EU-wide response is neither desirable nor appropriate. Sustainable systems and safe pensions can only be secured when each Member State has identified the policy changes required and established the necessary consensus for their implementation.

Despite the substantial differences in approach, Member States share crucial problems. As a result of population ageing, public expenditure could rise dramatically. Without reforms, the level of expenditure of state pension schemes could, in some Member States, reach 15-20 per cent of GDP in 2030. Unfunded pension liabilities could, in some cases, represent up to 200 per cent of GDP.[4] A large growth in the share of pensioners will inevitably require an increase in the resources set aside by the active population. The employment rates and productivity levels of the active generations will therefore be important determinants of the living conditions of the retired. All Member States have a need to modernise or adjust pensions systems and labour market practices so that they become mutually supportive and more conducive to the promotion of economic growth and social cohesion.

As the employment strategy has shown, a collective reflection at the EU level can help Member States to place the issues firmly on their internal policy agenda. An open exchange of experiences and ideas capturing the diversity of practices across the EU will broaden the range of policy options. Finally, by showing how adequate pension provision can be made sustainable, such co-operation, involving all actors, will help strengthen public confidence in pension systems.

Modernising and reforming pension systems is a complex process involving a broad range of interests and actors. The livelihood of a large and potentially vulnerable share of the population depends on this. It is necessary to respect legitimate expectations and to maintain an equitable and sustainable balance between rights and obligations. Reforms should be sufficient to meet the challenges ahead, credible, transparent and clear in their impact and should allow enough time for people to adjust. The reform process will require that all relevant actors be involved and committed to change. This makes it urgent to design comprehensive reform strategies long before acute financing problems will materialise.

The aim is, thus, to stimulate a joint effort which identifies practical ways of making adequate pension provision sustainable while maintaining sound public finances and intergenerational fairness. It is of considerable importance to the achievement of the overall strategic goal articulated at Lisbon that the Commission and the Member States should succeed in this objective. Conversely, by addressing all the factors, such as employment and economic performance, that influence pension systems, and not confining itself to the parameters of pension design, this Communication reaffirms that it is by means of the Lisbon strategy of mutually reinforcing social and economic policies that Europe can best hope to provide safe pensions and sustainable pension systems in the future.

Challenges To Pension Systems

Most of the resources available to older people are provided by pension systems. In the overall package of support to people after retirement, pensions represent the largest share, and the main source of pension income is public pension schemes. Old-age and survivors' benefits together represent nearly 45 per cent of total social protection spending in the EU, or around 12 per cent of GDP (see charts below)[5]. Most of the expenditure for old-age and survivors comes out of statutory pension schemes and is financed out of social insurance contributions and general taxation. In addition, as they are also the largest beneficiaries of health and long-term care, older people are the segment of society who are most dependent on social protection systems. The second largest item of social protection expenditure is health care which represents more than 7 per cent of GDP.

Social benefits by functions in 1997[6]

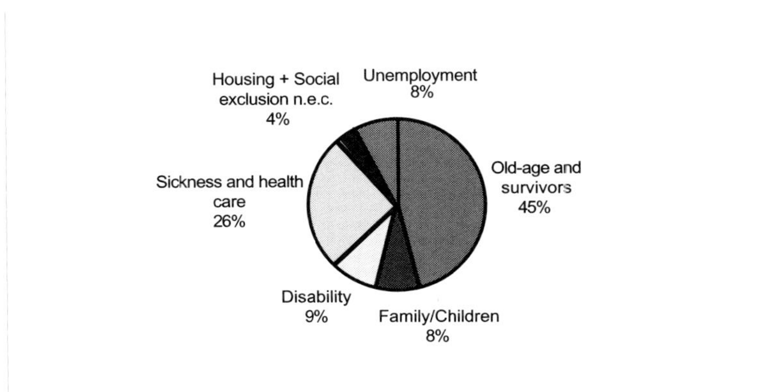

Old age and survivors benefits, 1997 (per cent 9f GDP)[7]

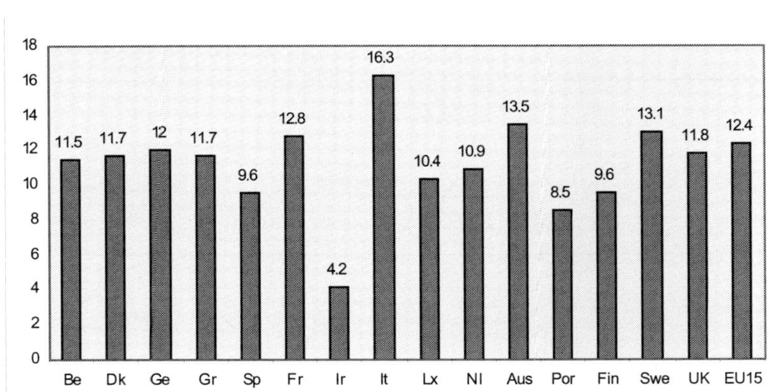

Over the past decades, Europe's pension systems have been remarkably successful in meeting their social objectives. Public pension provision has brought about a transformation in the income security and relative income position of old age pensioners. It has made older people independent and allowed them to enjoy a prolonged period of leisure after their working lives.

The risk of poverty in old age, once widespread, has been greatly reduced, and so has the number of people who have to rely on their descendants or means-tested social assistance benefits. Pension systems have achieved this in spite of a marked increase in life expectancy and in the number of pensioners over the past decades.

The biggest and most certain long-term challenge that confronts today's pension systems is demographic ageing. However, the need for reform of pension systems is not only related to the changing demographic balance. There is a critical interaction between financial sustainability of pensions, economic growth and employment which should not be neglected. On the one hand, higher economic growth and employment could open up new opportunities. Increasing the number of people in work is fundamental in order to stabilise or even reduce economic dependency ratios. On the other hand, pension systems need to perform better, both in terms of meeting their social objectives and supporting Europe's employment and growth objectives.

The implications of demographic change

Over the coming decades the number of older people will rise sharply in relation to people of working age. No reasonable policy measures will be able to counteract this change in the demographic structure of the European Union. However, it is not the demographic old-age dependency ratio that matters for the sustainability of pensions, but the economic dependency ratio.

Higher life expectancy due to higher welfare standards, better medical treatments and lower fertility rates are the driving forces behind a secular trend towards population ageing. This trend is not new and is set to continue. Medical progress shows no signs of decelerating, and past demographic forecasts have tended to underestimate the rise in life expectancy. Fertility rates are currently well below the level needed for a full replacement of the current population. A rise could occur if some of the existing barriers and disincentives to family formation and child bearing (related notably to labour market, housing and child care) are removed. Fertility rates tend to be higher in Member States implementing a sound policy of reconciliation of family and working life. However, they remain too low to prevent population ageing.

The major new development over the coming decades will be the large baby-boomer cohort, born after the end of World War II, reaching retirement age. This demographic bulge will initially be reflected in an ageing workforce, then, from 2010 onwards in a sharp increase in pensioner numbers and later in increased needs for health and long-term care.

The old-age dependency ratio will rise considerably over the next 30 to 40 years. According to Eurostat's long-term demographic projections, the number of working-age people per pensioner will halve by the year 2050 going from 3,5 to 1,8 at EU level (see table 1). The demographic effect of the post-war baby boom will start decreasing at around 2030 and is expected to disappear not earlier than the middle of the century.[8]

The rise in the number of older people will be such that the increase in the demographic old-age dependency ratio can neither be halted by a sudden increase in fertility nor by any realistic level of immigration. Changes in fertility only start having an impact on the labour market twenty years later. However, immigration can contribute towards raising the level of employment, but its positive impact depends on the extent to which migrants can be sufficiently integrated into the labour market.

Table 1: Baseline projections of old age dependency ratios in EU Member States (people aged 65+ years to people aged 20-64 years)

%	2000	2010	2020	2030	2040	2050
Belgium	29.5	31.1	38.0	48.8	53.5	52.0
Denmark	25.5	29.6	35.7	42.0	47.0	43.7
Germany	28.0	34.1	38.6	50.3	57.0	56.1
Greece	30.2	33.6	38.0	44.4	54.7	61.6
Spain	28.7	30.7	35.2	44.7	59.8	68.7
France	28.5	29.5	38.1	46.4	52.1	53.2
Ireland	20.3	20.5	26.2	32.1	38.4	46.6
Italy	30.7	35.5	42.1	52.9	67.8	69.7
Luxembourg	24.8	27.6	33.0	42.5	47.2	43.5
Netherlands	23.1	26.2	34.7	44.2	50.1	46.9
Austria	26.3	30.1	34.5	47.0	57.0	57.7
Portugal	26.7	28.5	32.2	37.2	46.3	50.9
Finland	25.9	29.7	41.4	49.5	49.7	50.6
Sweden	30.9	33.8	39.8	45.4	48.9	48.5
UK	27.8	28.5	33.9	43.1	49.1	48.5
EU-15	28.3	31.4	37.3	46.8	55.0	55.9

However, the sustainability of pensions depends not on the demographic dependency ratio but on how this translates into the economic dependency ratio (which is significantly higher) and transfer payments. It is therefore much more relevant for an assessment of the prospective sustainability of pension systems to consider the actual number of people in employment in relation to people who do not work. Currently, the economic dependency ratio (people aged 20 and over not in work as a proportion of total employed) is 0.86 in the European Union, which means that there are nearly as many working-age people who are not in work as people who are. Within the group of non-working adults nearly 6 out of 10 are below the age of 65, many of whom are in receipt of benefits of various kinds. The economic dependency ratio can be expected to be negatively affected by the rising old-age dependency ratio, but by reducing the number of inactive among the working-age population it will be possible to alleviate the financial burden of ageing that will have to be supported by the employed. Thus a crucial question is: to what extent it will be possible to counteract the impact of ageing on economic dependency rates by raising the overall employment rates?

Economic dependency ratios in 1999
Population 20 and over not in work as per cent of total employed

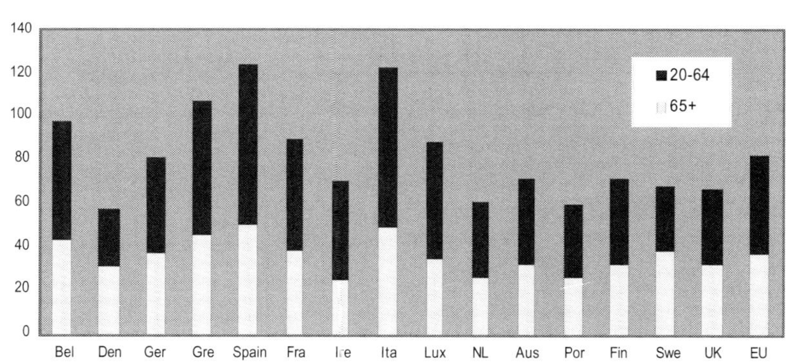

Political and economic dimensions of pensions reform

Reforms to make pension systems sustainable may well be politically difficult. They will need to achieve as large a consensus as possible. They must be comprehensive, not confined exclusively to pensions. A successful strategy for economic growth will be a major element of this. Maintaining sustainability of pensions in the face of rapid ageing implies a balance between contributions and entitlements and between the active and the retired populations. This presents a major political challenge.

A comprehensive strategy for securing adequate pensions in the face of demographic change can only be developed and implemented on the basis of consensus between and within generations. It is important that all relevant stakeholders be involved and committed. Such agreement should lead to more stability and predictability in pension systems.

Confidence in, and widespread acceptance of, pension systems are of crucial importance for their sustainability. Public, pay-as-you-go financed pension schemes have become the focus of widespread concern because the impact of ageing on these schemes is very direct and clear, whereas in the case of funded schemes the impact will be much more difficult to predict. Governments can alleviate these concerns by setting out a clear and credible strategy to ensure the sustainability of pension systems.

Sound macroeconomic policies and growth-enhancing structural reforms creating a favourable economic and business environment are critical for the future sustainability of pension systems. The integrated strategy articulated at the Lisbon Summit provides an excellent context for Member States to address this challenge.

Economic growth is a crucial determinant of public finances. Although many public pension schemes have dedicated sources of revenue in the form of social insurance contributions, general government contributions to all social protection schemes[9] generally represent nearly ten per cent of GDP for the EU as a whole. This link between general government budgets and the specific financing systems of pension schemes means that an uncontrolled rise in pensions expenditure might destabilise public finances. Conversely, the ability of governments to support pension schemes depends on other factors determining the soundness of public finances.

On the revenue side, a continued ability of governments to collect taxes and contributions is crucial. This may be affected by tax evasion, by cross-border differentials or by a higher mobility of tax bases and hence the possibility for economic activities to move to countries where the best balance between taxes/ contributions and public services can be found. The reduction of the overall tax burden, in particular on labour, to provide incentives to growth and employment is also to be taken into account. On the expenditure side, the evolution of other claims on public budgets will be important. In a context of sound macroeconomic policies and budgetary discipline the challenge will be to ensure that any rise in pension expenditure does not crowd out other legitimate claims on public budgets. One major current expenditure item is interest on government debt which should be reduced in preparation for ageing related cost. Sufficient preparations for a rise in ageing related costs should therefore be made.

Reliance on private, funded provision through occupational or personal pension schemes can be a useful tool to alleviate the burden on public finances. As a result the performance of financial assets becomes a more important determinant of older people's living standards. Financial market dynamics will be affected by demographic change with demand for financial assets increasing as a large cohort saves for retirement.

In many Member States, the process of reform is already well underway. A balance is being sought between the aim of providing sufficient and safe income to the elderly and that of making systems sustainable. While the measures introduced differ in detail, in practice, their common emphasis is on limiting the future transfers which will be necessary, particularly those which governments are responsible for, or increasing the finance available. They include increasing the official age of retirement or the number of years of contributions required to qualify for a full pension, reducing the pension paid in relation to past earnings, or relating it more closely to contributions, creating special funds to finance future transfers or encouraging the development of private, funded pension schemes.[10] These reforms could often benefit from being integrated in a more comprehensive strategy covering social protection reform, employment promotion and macroeconomic policies. The current healthy economic climate should be used as an opportunity for introducing comprehensive reforms.

The link between pensions sustainability, the Lisbon strategy and employment promotion

Current pension systems tend to encourage early exit from the labour market and are frequently used to reduce staff levels while avoiding redundancies. They often do not take into account differing individual needs. Some pension schemes offer insufficient coverage for the most mobile and flexible members of the workforce. More generally, the incentive structure of pension schemes needs to be reviewed to ensure that they become employment-friendly.

The European Council in Lisbon formulated an overall strategy for sustainable economic growth with more and better jobs and greater social cohesion. Demographic change means that a large workforce has to be achieved in a context of an ageing and shrinking population of working age. This will impose additional challenges across the entire range of economic, labour market and social policies cited by Lisbon. Pension systems need to be compatible with, and capable of, contributing positively to the realisation of all the elements of this strategy. The main challenges for pension systems in this regard relate to their interaction with labour markets. Pensions sustainability, but also the prospect of tightening labour markets and skill shortages in the future, makes it urgent to develop a strategy for mobilising society's full employment potential.

The conclusions of the Lisbon European Council established that, on the basis of a sustainable economic growth of 3 per cent of GDP, Member States should move towards a total average employment rate of 70 per cent, and over 60 per cent for women, in 2010. Employment growth of the sort we need to meet these objectives has a crucial role to play in ensuring the sustainability of pension systems. Clearly, other parameters may need to be adjusted at the same time (e.g. retirement age, level of contributions or the relative levels of pensions). Increasing the current levels of activity among women and older workers will be crucial. Reform of pension systems has a key role to play in this respect through the provision of better employment incentives.

Women's participation is clearly one key issue. Women still have particular problems in gaining equal access to the employment market, in career advancement, in earnings and in reconciling professional and family life. Although the net additional jobs created over the past decade or so have virtually all gone to women, this job growth has failed to keep pace with the increasing number of women who want to work and employment rates for women remain lower than for men. One reason for this are career interruptions to provide care. Such periods could receive a better recognition in pension systems. Adjustments should also be made to strengthen the incentives for women to enter, re-enter and remain in the labour market. Finally, the issue of individualisation of pension rights has to be considered in this context.

Another key issue is the premature exit of the older workers from the labour market. Today in most Member States the effective retirement age is well below the normal eligibility age in statutory pension schemes. One of the main reasons for this trend is that pension systems continue to offer substantial incentives for early retirement. In most pension systems, continuing to work beyond the first opportunity to retire entails having to pay social contributions without gaining extra pension rights. In addition, income from work may be taxed at a higher rate than pensions. Tax/benefit structures which subsidise early labour market exit while punishing people who work longer, undermine the principle of making work pay. Such structures not only lead to a waste of human resources and undermine the European Union's employment objectives, they also raise the cost of retirement systems substantially.

Table 2: Employment rates by age group in 1999

	Bel	Den	Ger	Gre	Spa	Fra	Irl	Ita	Lux	NL	Aus	Por	Fin	Swe	UK	EU15
50-54	60.3	80.4	73.4	60.1	57.2	74.1	62.1	57.2	64.6	70.2	72.7	71.4	78.9	84.2	75.9	69.2
55/59	36.9	70.9	55.1	47.4	44.8	46.8	50.5	36.6	38.2	49.6	41	59.1	54.6	77.8	62.1	50.7
60-64	12.9	34	19.6	30.4	24.7	10.1	35.9	17.9	12.9	18.6	11.7	43.6	22.2	47.9	35.6	22.3
65-69	3.8	6.2	5	11.5	3.9	2.1	14.3	6.2	n.a.	5.2	4.9	24.8	4.4	10.7	11.6	6.5

Source: Eurostat Labour Force Survey

The problem of early labour market exit is aggravated not only by the objective difficulties (such as out-dated skills) which older workers experience in finding reemployment after redundancy, but also by management practices which discriminate against them in the workplace and on labour markets. Under these conditions, early retirement schemes have often been regarded by employers, unions and workers as the only socially acceptable way of reducing staff levels. This age bias is often mirrored in practices within employment policies: older workers may find that they are barred from the placement, activation and training offers that are available to younger workers.

With ageing, pension systems will no longer be able to support the cost of shedding older workers whose skills are out-dated or because unhealthy working practices force them to retire early. Moreover, workers are increasingly fit enough to continue working until the official retirement age or even beyond if they so wish.

Reversing the trend towards early labour market exit will require providing stronger employment opportunities for older workers, reducing the disincentives for working longer in the form of early retirement options and other tax benefit structures while putting more emphasis on maintaining their employability. Pension systems will need to be adjusted in several ways to support working longer.

In this regard, today's fixed statutory retirement ages look increasingly inappropriate. They do not take account of rising life expectancy and the improved health status of most older people. Systems of flexible or gradual retirement had already been recommended by the Council in 1982.[11] They could be used to promote increased labour force participation and hence higher employment, thereby contributing to the long-term sustainability of pension systems.

Furthermore, promoting active participation should take account of the different categories of disadvantaged groups. In fact, an inclusive strategy does not only reduce the waste of human resources, it also helps containing some of the economic and social costs related to social exclusion liberating financial resources and helping the overall sustainability.

Pension systems must also be adapted so that they cater better for the needs of a more mobile and diverse workforce. In particular, any penalties for irregular career patterns or for mobility, either geographical or occupational, should be eliminated. Many occupational pension schemes, in particular, tend to impose substantial costs on people who change jobs or interrupt their careers.

In the longer term, Europe's job creation potential need not be limited by her current population size. It would be possible to attract immigrants, including well-qualified people, from third countries. Employment could rise further if birth rates went up again. While the determinants of fertility rates are clearly complex, more family-friendly workplaces and public policies that make it easier for parents to reconcile a professional career and family responsibilities could certainly play a positive role.

Mobilising society's full economic and social potential is the overriding policy requirement in the face of ageing. An integrated policy of technology driven productivity growth, more and better jobs and greater social cohesion, as articulated at Lisbon, provides the necessary framework for this mobilisation.

Ensuring adequacy and fairness in pension provision

Pensions have ensured that older people now enjoy reasonable living standards. However, there are still some gaps in income provision for older people. Poverty rates, especially among older women are higher than average. Granting pension rights for bringing up children or providing care is therefore an important element of solidarity in pension systems, as are lower contribution rates for low-paid workers. Present gaps in the adequacy and fairness of pensions call into question the Lisbon objective of creating greater social cohesion. It will be necessary to address such inadequacies which otherwise risk being aggravated in the context of ageing.

The average net adjusted[12] income of persons living in households receiving at least one pension (retirement or survivor's pension) is very close to average incomes of the population as a whole. Pension systems contribute around 60 per cent of the total net income of such persons. Other incomes include social transfers other than pensions, income from property and income from work (especially in those cases where pensioners share a household with people who are still in employment).

Relative equivalised income of persons living in households receiving pensions[13] (100 = all persons in a given country)[14]

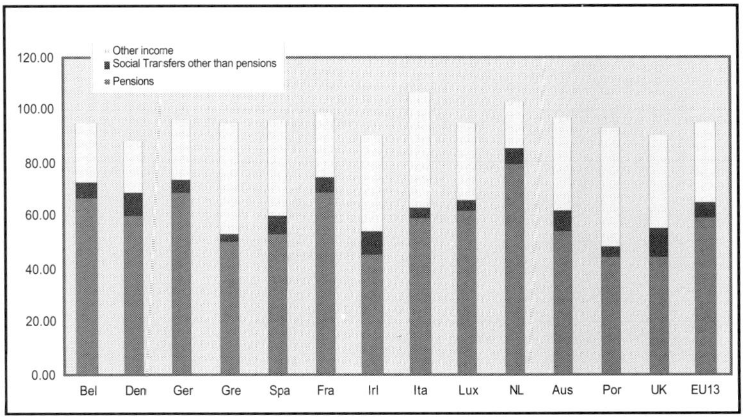

Despite this success, there are still cases in which pension systems fail to provide adequate minimum resources to the elderly. Older women, who constitute 2/3 of pensioners above the age of 75, are particularly prone to the risk of poverty in many Member States. In some countries, poverty rates are still higher among older people than in the total population, although the difference has narrowed. In the absence of minimum pension provision, short employment spells and career breaks often lead to inadequate pension provision, particularly in the case of women without adequate derived rights.

Growing labour market participation of women should result in a better protection in old age. However, women are still more likely to compromise their careers for family reasons and hence accumulate lower pension entitlements than their partners. As long as families are stable, pension systems may provide adequate protection through derived benefits.With increased family instability, the issue of sharing pension entitlement between spouses becomes more and more important.

Pension reforms will need to be carried out bearing in mind such inadequacies. In particular, expenditure cuts may not turn out to be as financially advantageous as expected if they lead to increased reliance on means-tested social assistance, thus shifting expenditure from pension systems to other social protection schemes. Surely, increased reliance on means-tested social assistance may contribute to expenditure cuts. However, means-tested social assistance and reliance on support from relatives may also undermine incentives to work (part-time after retirement from one's main job, or to earn income to meet the needs of elderly relatives) and to provide for one's own retirement (people on low incomes may not expect a pension above the social assistance level).

Pension reforms seeking to bolster the role of occupational and personal pension schemes will also need to address certain weaknesses of these schemes. Long vesting periods in occupational pension schemes make it difficult for people who are not part of a company's core workforce to earn sufficient pension entitlements. High management fees for personal pension plans can make them very unattractive to low-paid workers, and the practice of levying charges on initial contributions (front loading) imposes a high costs on scheme leavers. At EU level, the lack of coordination between such schemes, notably in the area of taxation, needs to be addressed to remove obstacles to cross-border mobility.

Strengthening the actuarial link between contributions and benefits (a measure which would strengthen the employment incentives in pension schemes) does not necessarily weaken solidarity. Many pension systems have redistributive elements in favour of the less-well off, for instance when they guarantee a minimum pension regardless of employment and contribution records or when contributions are levied on all incomes, but benefits are capped. On the other hand, pension systems may penalise manual workers (from an actuarial point of view) if pensions are calculated on the basis of final earnings or a number of years with high earnings without taking account of all contribution years and shorter life expectancy.

Managing Finance and Expenditure

A strategy for making pensions sustainable should focus on mobilising society's full potential[15] as well as on reforming pension systems themselves. By raising the employment rate of the working age population we can counter to a large extent the effect of demographic ageing on economic dependency ratios. This would ease the financial pressure on public pension schemes resulting from ageing and reduce the need for painful cuts in benefits or rises in contributions and taxes. A reform of pension systems is, however, necessary to make them conducive to employment creation and, in particular, encourage older workers to remain in the labour force. Implementing the Lisbon strategy will boost the ability of pension systems to respond to the challenges of adequacy.

In its progress report to the Feira European Council, the High Level Working Party on Social Protection suggested that an analysis of pension reform strategies should also consider how to manage finance and expenditure.

As pointed out before, this issue interacts with employment. On one hand, an effective way of raising more finance for pension schemes is to increase the number of contributors to them by increasing employment levels. On the other hand, reforming pension systems to improve labour market incentives will help to raise employment levels. Raising the real retirement age can result in very large savings provided increased expenditures in other areas can be avoided.

The study on sustainability of pensions will have to further analyse the various ways to secure a broader and stronger revenue base for pension schemes through diversification to alternative sources of finance, through the accumulation of fund assets and via the reduction of public debt. It will have also to analyse how to contain the rise in pension costs by improving efficiency and adjusting benefits while maintaining the social objectives.

Responding to the challenge of ageing calls for a comprehensive policy. In addition to sound macroeconomic policies and comprehensive structural reforms conducive to growth, higher employment and balanced public finances, the structure of public expenditure needs to be reassessed in order to ensure future growth and a generational balance in the distribution of public expenditure. In this context, reforms of current pension arrangements which secure adequacy and financial balance, while making schemes more employment-friendly are necessary. Reforms should result in durable solutions to the long-term problems and not just in stop-gap responses to imminent problems.

Guiding principles and objectives for pension reforms

It is for Member States to decide what pension system they want and what policy mix is required to maintain adequate incomes for older people without jeopardising the stability of public finances, undermining employment incentives or squeezing out other essential public expenditures. However, despite the considerable diversity within the European Union, Member States face common challenges which were analysed above. They also share common objectives with regard to pension systems and are committed to a number of principles, amongst which are equity and social cohesion which characterise the European social model. The Commission therefore invites Member States to co-ordinate their efforts and exchange views and information on practices and reforms in progress or at a planning stage. National choices and priorities in the strategies and detailed reform process do, however, remain the responsibility of Member States.

This cooperation among Member States can be made easier if common objectives and principles are made explicit. Clearly, tensions do arise between some of these objectives and principles, and Member States will have to strike a balance. Within the process set by the Lisbon Summit, the Commission presents the following principles and objectives to the discussion:

1. *Maintain the adequacy of pensions*: The three pillars of pension systems, operating in combinations decided by the Member States, should enable people to remain financially autonomous in old age and, within reasonable limits, to maintain the living standard achieved during their working life.

2. *Ensure intergenerational fairness*: The efforts needed to cope with demographic ageing should be shared in an equitable way between the active, be they employees or entrepreneurs, and the retired generations.

3. *Strengthen solidarity in pension systems*: No-one should be excluded from pension systems because of low-income or an unfavourable risk profile. Pension systems should have a redistributive element in favour of people with poor labour market opportunities or who had to provide care to children, disabled or frail elderly people.

4. *Maintain a balance between rights and obligations*: Benefits should reflect an individual's contributions to a pension system. In particular, postponing one's retirement should result in higher benefits.

5. *Ensure that pension systems support the equality between men and women*: In particular, adjustments are needed to strengthen the incentives for women to enter, re-enter and improve their position in the labour market.

6. Ensure transparency and predictability: It should be clear to pension scheme members what they can expect in terms of benefits under various circumstances.

7. Make pension systems more flexible in the face of societal change: Pension systems should be able to adjust to foreseeable changes in their economic and demographic environment.

8. Facilitate labour market adaptability: Pension systems should accommodate professional and geographic mobility and allow a degree of individual choice, for instance regarding the retirement age and the organisation of learning, working and leisure phases.

9. Ensure consistency of pension schemes within the overall pension system: Pension pillars should be mutually supportive and well co-ordinated.

10. Ensure sound and sustainable public finances: Reforms must ensure that the tax burden arising from public pensions is set at an appropriate level and that other essential public expenditures are not crowded out.

Next steps

Commission initiatives

In addition to the framework presented in this communication, the Commission will undertake the following initiatives to underpin this co-operative exchange on pension sustainability:

- In order to gauge public awareness and expectations regarding the modernisation of social protection systems, carry out, in the year 2001, a Eurobarometer survey on pensions and pension reform.
- Examine the relevant Community-wide statistical surveys with a view to ensuring that social protection issues in general and pension issues in particular are adequately covered.
- Propose an exchange of information on the issues covered in this Communication with the accession countries and, in the framework of its bilateral co-operation, the United States and Japan.

The Commission will also pursue its efforts to contribute to a better functioning of supplementary pension schemes:

- The proposal for a directive on the coordination of laws, regulations and administrative provisions relating to institutions for occupational retirement provision will allow private funded pension schemes to make the best use of investment opportunities, set high standards for the protection of beneficiaries and pave the way towards the cross-border management of occupational pension schemes. Enhancing the security and efficiency of these institutions and allowing them to fully benefit from the Single Market should contribute to the safety and sustainability of pension systems.[16]

• Further to its Communication *Towards a Single Market for Supplementary Pensions* of 11 May 1999 (COM(99) 134 final) the Commission will put forward an initiative dealing with the taxation of cross-border supplementary pensions early next year.

• The Pensions Forum, created following a suggestion by the High Level Panel on Free Movement, will consider how barriers to cross-border labour mobility related to supplementary pensions can be addressed.

Finally the Commission will take further initiatives on the future evolution of social protection with a view to supporting the co-operative effort on all objectives for the modernisation and strengthening of social protection as approved by the Council on 17 December 1999 (OJ 2000/C 8/7).

Setting up the framework of the study: The Lisbon request

As said in the introduction, the European Council at Lisbon requested the High Level Working Party on Social Protection '*to prepare a study on the future evolution of social protection from a long-term point of view, giving particular attention to the sustainability of pensions systems drawing on this communication.*' The High Level Working Party on Social Protection will submit a progress report on its work to the Nice Summit of December 2000.

The Commission proposes that the presentation of the challenges and policy responses discussed in this Communication should be used by the High Level Working Party on Social Protection as a framework for its ongoing work of analysis and exchange on pension reform issues.

The analysis to be carried out in this framework should be based, as far as possible, on harmonised data sources and hypotheses. In this context, the work undertaken by the Economic Policy Committee will be of a particular importance.[17]

Wherever possible, the approach should use longitudinal data taking into account all the related dimensions (demographic, economic, employment, social) and the interactions between them. In analysing future trends, the study should also take account of all the relevant policy objectives set at the EU level including the employment objectives set in Lisbon and the conclusions to be agreed in Nice.

The analysis should also benefit from the experience accumulated in the ongoing process of multiple reforms implemented in the Member States. The Commission suggests that the study serves as a basis for regular updating of information relating to pension reform in the Member States.

Finally the analysis should progressively include the candidate countries. The effectiveness and sustainability of schemes in new Member States integrating into the Union will be of common concern in economic and social terms. The reforms underway in candidate countries are of interest. These issues need to be given closer attention as the enlargement approaches while stressing that pension systems remain the responsibility of national authorities.

Notes

[1] Brussels, 11.10.2000 COM(2000) 622 final.
[2] This communication was presented to the Council of Ministers, the European Parliament and to the Economic and Social Committee.
[3] By Council decision of 29 June 2000 (2000/436/EC) a Social Protection Committee has been created. This Committee will replace the High Level Working Party.
[4] Commission communication *Towards a single market for supplementary pensions*, COM(99) 134 final. More up-to-date figures on public expenditure implications of ageing will shortly be presented by the Economic Policy Committee.
[5] These figures do not take account of taxes and contributions levied on social benefits. Such net social expenditure figures are difficult to calculate and are not yet widely available.
[6] Source: Eurostat, Esspros.
[7] Source: Eurostat, Esspros.
[8] The Economic Policy Committee's working group on the public expenditure implications of ageing, is currently engaged in developing projections of national public pensions expenditure relative to GDP up until 2050. Once ready, these will serve as broad indicators of the size of the demographic challenge as it affects public pension systems.
[9] Data on general government contributions to pension schemes only are not available.
[10] The Commission publishes regular reports on Member States' policies in the area of social protection. The latest one is: *Report On Social Protection In Europe 1999* (COM(2000) 163 final).
[11] Council Recommendation of 10 December 1982 on the principles of a Community policy with regard to retirement age (82/857/EEC), OJ L357, 18/12/1982, p. 27-28.
[12] The net income is adjusted per 'adult equivalent' to take account of differences in household size and composition: the income received by a household is divided by its 'equivalent size' computed using the modified OECD equivalence scale. Any member of a given household, child or adult, is assigned the same equivalised income.
[13] Source: European Community Household Panel, 3rd wave, 1996 (Eurostat, Statistics in Focus, Theme 3 – 9/2000, Social benefits and their redistributive effect in the EU.
[14] The average (equivalised) income of the whole population in a given country is put at 100. Pensions include retirement and survivor's pensions. For EU13, persons living in households benefiting from pensions have an average income of around 95 per cent. This means that their average standard of living, as measured by income, in 5 per cent lower than for the total population.
[15] The possible content of such a strategy in relation to ageing in general was discussed in COM(99)221 final 'Towards a Europe for all ages – Promoting Prosperity and Intergenerational Solidarity', which focussed on active ageing policies.
[16] Reference to COM document to be included (adoption foreseen for the same date as this communication).
[17] The Economic Policy Committee is working on the public finance implications of ageing. The aim is to provide a quantitative assessment of the public finance and economic consequences of ageing. Existing national expenditure projections have been reviewed and projections using common indicators and macroeconomic and demographic assumptions are being developed in co-operation with the OECD. Results will be submitted to the ECOFIN Council on November and made available to the High Level Working Party on Social Protection.

APPENDIX

Overview of national pension systems and recent reform measures[1]

Country	Main Features of pension systems (Pillars 1, 2 and 3)	Recent reform measures
Belgium	1. Earnings-related scheme. 2. Voluntary, mainly company-based schemes covering about 31 per cent of the working population. 3. Personal pensions available from life insurance companies or banks under favourable conditions.	Building on important reforms introduced in 1997 for private sector employees, the new government together with social partners is reflecting upon further reforms to cover for public sector employees and the self employed. Consideration is also being given to promote private funded pensions.
Denmark	1. Flat-rate public scheme based on residency/employment and contribution financed supplementary scheme with benefits linked to duration of employment (ATP). 2. Mainly sector-wide schemes based on collective agreements covering about 80 per cent of the working population. 3. Personal pensions available from life insurance companies or pension funds under the same tax conditions that apply to 2nd pillar schemes.	The transformation a largely unfunded system to one with a much higher degree of funding has been underway for some years. 1999 saw a temporary contribution to the ATP (Labour market supplementary pension) amounting to 1 per cent of the average wage made permanent and a tightening up of early retirement rules.

Country	Main Features of pension systems (Pillars 1, 2 and 3)	Recent reform measures
Germany	1. Earnings-related scheme. 2. Voluntary, mainly company-based schemes. 3. Personal pensions available from life insurance companies.	Pension reform was very high on political agenda. A tax reform package was agreed enabling increased revenues from energy taxes to partially offset a reduction in the contribution rate to pensions by employees and employers. Changes were also agreed for 2000/2001 linking increases in public pensions to inflation rather than the evolution of net wages. However, important reforms agreed in 1998 and due to come into force in 1999 were suspended by the new Government for two years, pending important reforms due to be announced in 2000.
Greece	1. Earnings-related scheme. 2. Voluntary, mainly company-based schemes covering about 5 per cent of the working population. 3. Personal pensions available from life insurance companies.	A two phase reform strategy was announced in 1998. The first phase was largely organisational, involving for example the introduction of single social security number. The second phase requires a major overhaul of public pensions, and could involve the consolidation of retirement ages in different pension regimes, adjusting contribution and eligibility rates to sustainable levels, and the introduction of compulsory occupational pension scheme. Announcements on the second phase are still being awaited.
Spain	1. Earnings-related scheme. 2. Voluntary, mainly company-based schemes covering about 5 per cent of the working population. 3. Personal pensions available from life insurance companies and pension funds.	Important reforms were introduced in 1997 (based on the 1995 Pacto de Toledo) which placed public pensions on a more sustainable footing. Further reforms are scheduled for 2000. They will need to address measures to increase the effective retirement age and discourage early retirement, and special pension regimes (e.g. covering self-employed, agricultural workers). In 2000, minimum pensions will increase by between 5.4 and 16 per cent depending on the type of pension, though on average by only slightly above 5.4 per cent. In 2000 a Social Security fund reserve has been created to address the problem of the ageing population . The initial fund amounts to 0.1 per cent of GDP and there is a commitment in the updated Spanish Stability Programme to further increase this fund reserve.

Country	Main Features of pension systems (Pillars 1, 2 and 3)	Recent reform measures
France	1. Earnings-related schemes. 2. Compulsory, pay-as-you-go financed occupational scheme based on cross-sectoral collective agreement, some additional, mainly company-based voluntary schemes. 3. Personal pensions available from life insurance companies under favourable tax conditions.	After postponing reforms adopted in 1997, a report was presented in 1999 to serve as a basis for dialogue between authorities and social partners which is now taking place. Reforms are scheduled for 2000 and could include measures to raise the effective retirement age, whether special pension regimes need to be brought in line with the general regime , and possible strengthening of a Social Security reserve fund which was established in the 1998 budget.
Ireland	1. Flat-rate scheme based on contributions. 2. Voluntary, mainly company-based schemes covering about 50% of the working population. 3. Personal pensions available from life insurance companies under similar tax conditions to those that apply to 2nd pillar schemes.	In May 1998, the Government outlined its plans for creating a fully developed pension system. As part of the 1999 budget, an annual provision of 1 per cent of GDP will be made to pre-fund future public pension costs. This fund was supplemented with part of the proceeds from the privatisation of the State telecom company. Part of the proceeds were also use to buy-out the State s future pension liabilities to pre-privatisation staff.
Italy	1. Earnings-related scheme 2. Schemes based on collective agreements for a company, a group of companies or an industry. 3. Personal pensions available from open pension funds and from life insurance companies under favourable tax conditions.	A series of reforms in the 1990s, the last one in 1997, have contributed to stabilise the ratio of pension expenditure to GDP in the medium term, but it remains high. The main weaknesses of past reforms are excessively long transition periods, excessive generosity, and uncertainty about future reforms. No reforms were undertaken in 1999.
Luxembourg	1. Earnings-related scheme. 2. Voluntary, mainly company-based schemes covering about 17 per cent of the working population. 3. Personal pensions available from life insurance companies.	Reforms were introduced in 1998 to align the pension regime for new public servants with that applying to the private sector.

Country	Main Features of pension systems (Pillars 1, 2 and 3)	Recent reform measures
Netherlands	1. Flat-rate scheme based on residency/employment. 2. Mainly sector-wide schemes based on collective agreements covering about 90 per cent of the working population. 3. Personal pensions available from life insurance companies under favourable tax condition.	With a large proportion of pensions already funded, the impact of ageing populations is Being addressed via the reduction of public debt and measures to increase employment rates.
Austria	1. Earnings-related scheme. 2. Voluntary, mainly company-based schemes covering about 11 per cent of the working population. 3. Personal pensions available from life insurance companies.	Large reform packages were adopted in 1993 and more recently in 1998. The latter reform addressed incentives for early retirement, tightened up eligibility for disability pensions, and aligned the pension system for civil servants to the general system. Also an annual adjustment formula was introduced making an adjustment for the financial impact of increased life expectancy. This was, however, suspended in 1998 and 1999 and must be addressed in 2000.
Portugal	1. Earnings-related scheme. 2. Voluntary, mainly company-based schemes covering about 7 per cent of the working population insured under the general social security system. 3. Personal pensions available from life insurance companies and pension funds.	A new framework law was presented by the new Government in late 1999 in response to a White Paper presented in 1999. Reforms are therefore expected to be adopted in 2000. Inter alia, it will need to address the creation of a compulsory second pillar contributory based scheme, and tackling early retirement.
Finland	1. Flat-rate public scheme based on residency. 2. Compulsory occupational schemes (pay-as-you-go and funded) and additional voluntary schemes. 3. Personal pensions available from life insurance companies.	During 1999, agreement was reached between labour market organisations on measures to postpone early retirement and extend active participation. Together with a large primary balance, this will make it easier to meet increased age-related expenditures in coming years. However, questions remain about the long-term sustainability of existing public pension schemes, and further reforms are likely to be required to tackle imbalances at source.

Country	Main Features of pension systems (Pillars 1, 2 and 3)	Recent reform measures
Sweden	1. Earnings-related scheme. 2. Mainly sector-wide schemes based on collective agreements covering about 90 per cent of the working population. 3. Personal pensions available from life insurance companies or banks or through direct capital market investment.	Reforms adopted 1998 are currently being phased in. They are increasing the degree of funding pensions. They also establish a closer link between contribution paid and benefits received, and indexation clauses were adjusted.
United Kingdom	1. Flat-rate scheme based on contributions and state earnings related pension scheme (SERPS). 2. Voluntary, mainly company-based schemes. Can be used as a substitute for SERPS and cover about 46 per cent of the working age population. 3. Personal pensions available from life insurance companies. Can be used as a substitute for SERPS.	Projections released in 1999 show a broadly sustainable long-term position for the UK's public finances. Extensive reforms were proposed in late 1998 and adopted in 1999. They provide for a minimum income guarantee and a replacement of SERPS (state earnings related pension scheme) with a second flat rate pension.

[1] Sources: DG MARKT, *Study on pension schemes of the Member States of the European Union, May 2000*, for the column 'main features of pension systems', Report from the Commission on the implementation of the 1999 Broad Economic Policy Guidelines (COM(2000) 143 final) for the column 'recent reform measures. More detailed information is available in Report on Social Protection in Europe 1999 (COM(2000) 163 final) and *MISSOC – Social protection in the Member States of the European Union*, DG EMPL, annual publication.